More Opic Observations

by

Jack Haines

Published by Rogue Phoenix Press
Copyright © 2014
ISBN: 978-1-62420-101-

Credits

Cover Artist: Designs by Ms G

And

Rogue Phoenix Press

Copyright 2014

Table of Contents

▶ Jack Haines

Ruth, I thank you for your patience.

Jack

More Opic Observations

LIFE VERSUS ART

Life versus Art.
Chicken versus Egg.
Betty versus Wilma.
All are serious, never ending debates of time. Let's look at just one debate right now.

Which imitates which? I am certain students of Art will say Art imitates Life. One can see how Art can be intricate and beautiful, bold and harsh just like Life. Art shows us the complexity of man and the simplicity. Paintings, stories and music try to depict man as he is and how he differs from other creatures.

Then there are those who believe, sometimes, Life imitates Art. These would be the incidents where people have an urge to take on impossible tasks with a quixotic fervor to right the wrongs that confront us.

Then there is television.

First we have to assume television is an art form. If television exhibits an art form, it is not Art in and of itself, no more so than a theater or museum is Art. "Unscripted" (Reality) Television would have to be the Art we are looking at.

Now that we are divided and confused, please analyze this: Many people think Reality Television began as a way around paying real writers to write screenplays for broadcast. It happened early on in the history of television. The broadcast companies had smaller budgets back then and had to cut corners where they could.

1

This is where they would dilute the reality of Reality TV.

How many can remember in the fifties when a television show began that would pit *Contestants* against each other? No, not a sports show. This show would have four ladies compete against each other by telling their terribly sad stories of their terribly sad lives.

The studio audience would applaud to determine the winner of the game. She would be the woman who had the worst situation and how the only way to spin around her bad luck would be to receive a truckload of name brand household appliances. The same name brand appliances were the sponsors of the program.

Hmmm.

This show was called *Queen For A Day*. Every day there would be four new ladies, four new sad stories and a new truckload of name brand appliances. It was one of the first non-sports related reality shows on television. The show was very popular and ran for years. Most people have forgotten this show; it was a long time ago.

These are the people you see on local news every day, especially around Christmas, who seem to proudly display their dumb luck, stupidity or guile on the news.

They are standing in their driveway. They are wearing a tee-shirt that states their love for their local middle school. They solemnly state they lost their entire Christmas from the back of their station-wagon that had the motor running. They can't understand how in just the time it took to run their lucky lottery numbers, someone stole their Christmas.

The clever news team can always find something at the scene to focus on; a broken window or muddy boot prints or fir needles on the floor next to an angel crying because there will be nothing under her dress this year. The news story always ends with the victims palms up, shrugging their shoulders with that far-away look in their eyes. Eyes holding back tears from someone who forgot to lock their front door or put their stuff in the trunk or close the car door.

What are they to do?

The answer is, they will go home and wait by the phone so it can ring to give them the Christmas they would never have. They have done everything they needed to do by being on television. The rest is up to you, the public, to respond to their puzzlement as to what will happen to them now. They will spend the next few days receiving the Christmas they *lost*.

A follow-up interview will show them crying tears of thanks for the dozens, I mean, several people who helped them out. It will show them locking their front door or turning off the engine of their new SUV or hugging their child wearing their new Abercrombie and Fitch shirt. They also could be seen locking up their new storage unit that holds next year's Christmas.

So you see Life, in this case, is imitating Art. Although we have to except *Queen For A Day* as Art. Maybe next week we will tackle that *Chicken/Egg* thing and someday, after some beer, we'll talk *Betty/Wilma.*

3

- -

REMEMBERING MY HOMETOWN

I was talking to Jeff, a childhood friend, at a baseball game the other day. We started talking about our hometown. We agreed on many opinions we shared about the old burg. We are probably far enough along in our lives where we can talk out loud about our shared experiences. We lived in the cutest little all white towns in our cute little mostly white state.

You would think, if a town, back in the fifties, sixties and seventies was all white they would be happy with that. Well, these people must have had more time on their hands because just being white was not quite enough for them. Our melting pot must have been in the dishwasher at that time.

As I think about it now, we didn't have obvious groups of people that would stick out in a crowd. There were no special holiday events dedicated to any particular group of people. No St. Patrick's Day parade, No Sons of Norway Days, no Happy Anybody Days. In fact, no Happy. We didn't sing Happy Birthday. We took pride in our sternness.

As kids, we didn't see this, of course. We had fun in our apparent sameness and secretly smiled at each other. At the beginning of the seventies, our town began to change. Our town began an annual parade and sidewalk sale.

This was put on by the Chamber of Commerce and turned into a function that survives to this day. It was a record-breaking event. First of all, it was the first parade held during the day, no dangerous torches. The parade went all the way through town, not just stopping at in front of the courthouse like in the old days.

The Grand Marshall was someone everyone knew and liked and he lived through the process of the parade. In fact, he was in many parades to come. He smiled, waved and was happy.

I guess I always had an uneasy feeling about things back then, but I couldn't quite put my finger on it. When I was talking with Jeff the other day, it started to come back to me. Since I left the area right after high school, I had other things to think about. I put much of my past in one of those little boxes in my brain, I left it there and it stayed frozen in time. I think it was freeze-dried, you know, like Tang, because we brought it out and added a little beer and it was back as big as day.

It started to make me think about stuff I was afraid to think about in the sixties. We lived in a bad town. I should have picked up on it back then. Why didn't I see it?

Jeff and I spoke in hushed whispers, even though we were miles away from our old town. As we brought up item after item, they fit together like pieces of a puzzle. It was indeed a bad town. It seems, not only did you have to be white to live in our town; you had to belong to the right church. We didn't.

Apparently, our church was competing for God's attention. You know how simple God can be. This was not good for the town. In the old days, we would have led the parade. It would have been held in our honor because of us. This would make things in the town good again. God would have an easier time seeing them without being distracted by our religion. I should have known better. I thought my mom was just paranoid. We really were persecuted.

This started a small thinking process on my part. It seems I do have a point of reference on the topic of discrimination. I thought I was just sensitive to others. I lived through learning how to answer questions without answering exactly.

"What church do I go to...? Er... You know, it's white; white inside and outside, small cross near the top someplace. You know..."

I got a job, early in my teens. This saved me from making excuses why I couldn't attend Vacation Bible School last week. Now, I remember.

This thinking I did last week made me examine how acceptance works, maybe. In the last one hundred sixty years, the people of our country have accepted many different peoples. Nationwide, we overcame the fear of Irish, Italians, Jews, Blacks and Hispanics.

I know this may sound like an over simplification of how things work, but please follow me. This makes sense, kind of. Each of these groups suffered discrimination in our country for some time, but eventually became accepted, maybe because of baseball. Baseball, of all the pro sports, was the most progressive. Yes, the road was rocky for many of the first pioneers. It took strong individuals as well as talented ones to overcome a complete nation; a nation of scared people. They were scared that maybe Jackie,

Willie, Yogi or A-Rod might distract God from looking at them for a minute. You know how simple God can be.

Maybe I only connected the dots the way I did because we were at a baseball game, but it did make sense.

We had little league in the old days but it wasn't the *Bigs,* and we only could watch televised games on Saturday and during the World Series. The little town now has cable and satellite and I am certain by now the town folk could probably accept ideas and concepts that would have been shot on sight or the focus of a torch lit parade.

Jeff said his sister sent him an email. There is an Irish family moving in to our old neighborhood, you know, in Sternville.

It sounds like they might have rounded a corner.

- -

RANDOM OBSERVATIONS

The following are images that came to me at various times.

I once thought about selling my observations, then I heard the newspapers pay by the inch; another example Big Business is putting it to the little guy. The bastards!

I sit in front of the computer all day and write this stuff. Thankfully, my wife thinks I'm just looking up porn.

I watch a lot of TV. They say it's detrimental to your intellect. I don't get it.

When I write, I listen to TV. I thought I just heard: *Free puppy to the first homeless family to come in to the Humane Society.* "Because, you have so much in common."

My wife tells me I need a hearing exam. I like hearing things the way I do.

I was driving past the homeless shelter last week. I stopped behind a school bus. As her third grader got on the bus, I thought I heard the mother say, "Bye, Bobby. I'll see you tonight when you get...not home." I could be wrong.

Last night I was sitting next to a guy in a bar, he was quite a ways ahead of me in the consumption department. He wanted to show me pictures of all his girl friends on his cell phone. I said no thank you.

Wilma and Betty. Ginger and Maryann. Catherine Willows and Sara Sidle. Is it just me?

I had a molar extracted last week. Now I talk with a lisp and when I floss, the sink fills up with Cheerioth.

Christmas has been over for a pretty long time now. I hope I don't forget the words to those carols. My wife said I can no longer wear my Baby Jesus suit in public. Apparently it's inappropriate.

Maybe George Bush was right, some people do hate our religion.

~ * ~

I thought I saw this on TV:

ITC (Interstate Technical College)—A new television ad:

"Crime rates are higher than ever! Citizens are afraid to go outside!" states a rich baritone voice. "Take advantage of these facts by enrolling today at ITC."

A still photo shows students in lab coats and safety glasses. "Learn crime solving techniques and up-to-the-minute forensic abilities to thwart crime in your community."

The next image shows the trim waist and gun belt of a uniformed officer. The voice continues. "ITC graduates are now standing shoulder to shoulder in your neighborhood. With their new-found knowledge, students are scouring the landscape for tell-tale signs of invasive security cameras and remembering from their intense education to always wear gloves, keep your head down and wear a dark hooded sweatshirt. Because even though some ITC graduates land good jobs in law enforcement or Fox News, the rest still have to find a way to pay their ITC tuition bill and with their new ITC education, they now know how."

~ * ~

New product ad: INFLATABLE POPE
Life size, life-like, inflatable Pontiff dressed in realistic (Away) vestments. He has movable legs so he can sit or stand and movable arms so he can wave or bless passer-byes. Imagine sitting with The Pope in your own den, watching TV and drinking a beer. Take him to church with you; your friends will envy you forever. Available with 9-volt tape recorder and speaker. Let The Holy Father help you with fund-raising. "B-Zwei." Buy the twelve volt electric or pedal powered air pump for quick and easy inflation. Order the vinyl patch kit, in case of accidental puncture or an assassination attempt, just in case. The Pope can be deflated and stored in his handy carrying case that resembles The Pope Mobile.
He's infallible, He's inflatable, He's The Pope and He's all yours for only four easy payments of $99.95.
(A product of Golden Calf Products: "If it's a Golden Calf, you'll love it!")

~ * ~

You would think if people have an idea on how to take advantage of a situation, they might think it all the way out. At the risk of sounding like

Navin Johnson, I also look forward to the arrival of the new phone book. I understand how the phone book works. If your name is first in a line of people providing a particular service, people are more likely to call you than go through all of the septic tank evacuation specialists in the book. A-1 PUMPERS has a better chance of getting a call than ZEB'S HONEY DIPPERS.

Some people try to out think the phone book searcher. For example they place additional A's ahead of their name so they can be ahead of others in their category. A classic ploy is A-1 PUMPERS. This may not be the best idea if, for example, you thought you would get more calls if you change your listing to—A.A.ADAMS, SPEECH THERAPIST.

~ * ~

I thought I heard this was a new show on TV this fall.

HUNCH PUPPIES on The Animal Channel —"Two young dog brothers solve crimes that baffle the authorities by using their intuitive powers."

The premise is laid out by a voice-over announcer. Film clip shows the dogs at the Sheriff's office.

The Sheriff asks, "How did you boys know the butler did it?"

Sparky says, "We just had a feeling. You see, we are intuitive"

All three, "HA! HA! HA!"

11

~ * ~

I thought I heard this on the news.
"Thanks to the success of certain theme parks in the South and looking to open up to more groups of people, the Lottery Board plans to unveil its new line of scratch off themes:

BIBLE STORIES

Old Testament Giants vs. New Testament Heroes

Scratch-off game closely resembling Tic-Tac-Toe only using Rocks and Crosses.
Adam and Eve—The Sratch-off Years
Match three like symbols and win cash!: Apple, Fig Leaf, Lightning Bolt, God's Head. Caution: Don't uncover the Snake, you'll lose!

Noah's Barque

Scratch-off game where you must match animals; 1 male, 1 female. You could win a boat!

Guess Nebuchadnezzar's Age

Scratch-off the three correct digits.

Apostle AKA

Match the Apostle with his Apostle nickname. Example: Peter (Big Peter), James (Jimmy the Kid), Thomas (Mr. Gullible), Matthew (Stinky)

Holy Craps!

Scratch-off game reveals dice totaling seven: Win a Jesus Suit (Autographed).

~ * ~

"You don't have to butter coat it for me. I'm not an idiot, you know!"

~ * ~

List of jobs I thought about but for one reason or another I decided not to follow-up on:
Key Grip on movie being shot next week; "Fast and Curious, Too".
Doggie Stylist at the new pet groomers' shop.
Product development specialist for 1/3 scale "Baby's First Toys":
Alternative Store specialty; "Baby's First Bong".

~ * ~

My wife just returned from the grocery store. She was looking confused.
"What's the matter?"
"I just ran into my friend Brenda at the store."
"The girl you went to school with?"
"Yeah."
"How is she doing?"
"I don't know. She kind of creeped me out."
"Really? What happened?"

13

- -

"She was wearing her winter coat and it had a beautiful broach pinned to the lapel. I told her I thought it was beautiful and very unique."

"Yes?"

"She said it was a family heirloom. I said how interesting and asked her from where her family originates. She spun on her heels and said she didn't think we knew each other enough to be asking questions like that."

"What? This was your friend from fourth grade?"

"Yes, that's what's so weird. You know, I haven't seen her for some time."

"Maybe she has something to hide. Maybe she's from another planet."

"Yeah, Planet Stupider."

~ * ~

I heard they opened up a new restaurant in town. It's for Bacotarians. It is called the Bacotorium. They serve bacon from all fifty states. The Baconista puts together your order. You order bacon by the slice. Side orders include eggs, toast, pancakes, biscuits and gravy.

Dessert items include bacon wrapped cupcakes, bacon chip cookies and bacon milk shakes.

The owners said they have always wanted to show how bacon is different from state to state. They spent years traveling across the country eating local foods. They decided their love for bacon is what inspired them to open this type of restaurant.

~ * ~

Chicken fried steak but not steak fried chicken.

~ * ~

Animals wearing clothes, very funny. People wearing no clothes, not so funny.

~ * ~

We are really enjoying our retirement. We are doing things we couldn't do or didn't do while we were working, just doing it slower. Remember when everyone went skinny dipping in college. I do. I had to work that day. Today, my wife and I can go to any nude beach and it's unbelievable, as soon as we spread out our blanket and I start my stretching exercises, the rest of the people pack up and give us the whole beach on which to frolic. Now that's respect!

Another sign of respect we encounter today is when we go bowling. We enjoy bowling. If we go bowling, and it's crowded, we find the kindness of others always touches us. When we try to squeeze in between two large parties, the noise subsides. They must know how much noise can be a distraction to us. For example, yesterday just as we sat down to change our shoes, the family next to us decided to suspend their game. The children began pleading with their parents. Tears streamed down their little faces as they gasped and gulped air. They insisted we play and they would sit in the car and wait until we were done.

"Be sure and crack the window, honey", my wife made a circular cranking motion in the air. "It's supposed to get ninety-seven degrees today." She is ever the grandmother.

The mother covered her face with a Kleenex and began asking my wife questions that I could not hear.

"No, we're not wearing Ben-Gay. Jack just has a dab of an analgesic cream based ointment. It's for his back. Why do you ask, Honey?"

~ * ~

Door to Door Social Dating Network

~ * ~

"The Senator is holding a press conference in the Dodgeitorium, Sir".

ANOTHER CASE OF WRITER'S BLOCK

My wife, Ruth, and I were having dinner the other evening when she asked me. "What's wrong?"

I must have had a pained look on my face. "Huh?"

"You are looking through that wall."

"I'm sorry, I can't think about anyone interesting enough to write about."

"Are you kidding?"

"Well…"

"What about that girl we met at the pizza parlor last week?"

"You might have to be more specific," I replied.

"The girl told us the story about her friends who got stabbed because they were standing on their porch minding their own business."

"Oh, yeah, it makes you wonder, what are things coming to?"

Then she added, "Well what about the kid at the restaurant that does the bus-work, the one who wears the Buddy Holly glasses?"

"Oh, you mean Bobby? He's okay; his brother is a little sketchy."

"They're twins!" She rolled her eyes.

"Right."

We finished our meal.

"Let's go have a quick beer; we have time before our favorite show." Ruth knows a beer is a good catalyst for getting hold of my Muses.

17

- -

"Okay, but you're driving." There was really no reason for me to say that since she always drives. She is a better driver and it gives me an opportunity to look around as we drive through our neighborhood. I figure I look like a big dog gawking out of the passenger window. I try to remember to keep my tongue in my mouth. I urge her to drive faster so the wind can blow my hair around.

"Get your head back inside!"

"Grrr."

Our hideout is very busy tonight. There is no place to sit.

As we look around, a guy I have never seen before approaches me.

"If you don't mind, you folks can sit with me. I have a table and I feel guilty being be myself with this big table when they are so busy."

It sounded good to me so I motion to my wife. She joins us and we introduce ourselves. I immediately forget his name; Jason, Jimmy, Josh, New Guy? Okay, his name probably isn't New Guy. Oh well.

We sit down and exchange small talk. New Guy says this is his second time at our hideout. We point out some of the features: nice bar, friendly staff, local color, loud music. It is quite noisy tonight; someone must be having a birthday or getting ready to go to Confession tomorrow.

New Guy leans forward as he speaks. He has a faraway stare as though he is trying to remember if he took his meds this week. His hands are folded and placed on the table before him. His face is red from working out in the sun all day. "I started my garden today."

"Oh really, Randy?" My wife is always polite.

"I rototilled my garden space, it took me all morning. It's as big as this room."

"About forty by eighty? That's pretty good size." I was impressed she knew the size of the room.

"Well, you'll probably feel that tomorrow," I added.

"It took longer than I thought. The rototiller kept getting clogged and I had to stop and clean out the…"

"Tines?"

"No, those blades on the bottom."

"You didn't knock down last year's crop?" Ruth is a veteran of many a garden and knows all the steps and reasons for them. "You know last year's crop should have been burned in place before you rototilled."

This information flew at least three feet over his head.

"What are you going to plant?" She asked.

"Squash and pumpkins, ma'am."

"They'll take up a lot of room but it sounds like you have plenty. Place three seeds per hole and quit watering after the fruit has formed. That goes for tomatoes too."

"Are you going to plant potatoes?" I asked. I remember harvesting potatoes and slicing them fresh and throwing them in the Fry Daddy.

"Oh, no sir, I just want some corn. I'm going to plant it on the south side of the garden."

"You don't want to do that; if you do that, the corn would shade the rest of your garden. You want to put the corn on the north side of the garden."

"But the street is on the South side of my garden."

Now, I'm getting confused. He still has that faraway look on his face. "Are you okay, Buddy?"

"Yeah, I'm just a little dizzy."

No shit.

"After I got done today, I drank a half bottle of Tequila with my uncle then I drank the other half by myself."

He also must be getting up enough nerve to go to Confession.

"You better eat some food, man. We'll leave you alone now. We have to go back home."

"Thanks for hanging out with me. See you, folks."

"See you, New Guy!"

"Thanks for sharing your table with us, Randy."

"Show off."

On the way back home my wife says, "That ought to shut you up."

"What?"

"You could write about that guy all night."

"He was a bit odd."

"Odd? He was nuts. When you went to the restroom, he told about the time he came here last week. He was outside and he started a conversation with a ten year old girl."

"Ewww, that's spooky."

"He talked to her for an hour. He said they had a lot in common."

"I can probably write about it, but I'll have to wash my hands when I get done."

"Get your head back inside and quit sticking out your tongue."

THE NINE O'CLOCK TO MANKATO

"Francie, wake up! Someone is here." Her grandmother was shaking her awake and whispering in her ear.

"What? Who is it?" was whispered back by the fifteen-year old, waking up quickly, her eyes flashed in fear.

"I don't know, but Teddy is barking like crazy. Someone is coming to the door."

Francie lived with her grandmother since she was thirteen. Her parents and brothers lived down the road. Grandmother was widowed and lived alone on the old family farm.

It was two o'clock in the morning. The girl and her grandmother were frightened being in the big farmhouse by themselves. They knew it was something serious because the hair of the mixed-breed shepherd dog was standing straight up on his neck; his nose pressed on the front window as he was growling and bearing his teeth.

They hid in the dark looking at the front entrance. The moonlight was shining through the window next to the door and caused an eerie glow.

The screen squeaked open. Their hearts stopped as they heard a loud rap on the glass of the front door, one, two, three raps.

"Mary! Open up! It's me, George!"

"George? What are you doing here at this time of the night?"

"I need to talk to Francie right now!"

"Just a minute, George. Teddy, it's okay. Good boy!" She snapped a stare back to Francie, still hiding in the dark. In the stare was also an eye raised in question, as if it asked her what she did. Mary reached for the key in the door lock and turned it to the left, it clicked and the door opened. Teddy growled again. "It's okay, Teddy! It's just George."

"Where's Francie? I've got to talk to her!"

"She's right here, George. What's the matter? It's two o'clock!"

Francie moved closer to the door as her grandmother turned on the light in the living room.

"Francie, where are the boys?"

"George, how would Francie know where the boys are? We've been here all night, just the two of us."

"She knows. She's always with them, that's how I know. They are always together, the four of them."

It was true. They were inseparable: Leonard, Georgie, Frankie and Francie. They were within two years of each, other but they grew up together and did everything together. They went to school together; they played together and skated on the lake together in the winter. It was natural, they were cousins and actually, Frankie and Francie were brother and sister. Leonard and Georgie were their cousins, one from their mom's side and one from their dad's side.

It was not unusual for teens in the 1930s to group together for entertainment and protection. Although they lived by the lake their entire life and knew everyone in their enclave, there were not many options for the young during the depression in the small village by the Mississippi.

"Francie, do you know were the boys are?"

"No, Grandmother. I was with you all night."

"You know where they are, girl! It's two o'clock in the morning and my Georgie is not home, the same with Leonard and your brother, Frankie. I know. I checked and I called Sheriff Dieter."

Oh no, this is serious, thought Francie. She remembered the scary big man from last fall when he was campaigning for sheriff. He drove his truck around the county with a keg of beer in the back "getting to know" the constituents over a friendly beer. Her heart began pounding and her face got red, she was ready to cry.

"I can't tell. I promised," she hoarsely whispered. Her mouth was too dry to help her talk.

"What ?!"

Now she was crying. She sobbed as her grandmother held her close.

After what seemed like an hour to her uncle, she gathered some composure.

George said something in German that the girl could not understand.

Her grandmother said, "No, George!" in English.

Francie wiped her eyes with the back of both of her hands. "They ran away from home." There, she said it. She betrayed her brother and her cousins. She was in on it from the beginning and had she not backed out at the last-minute, she too would be a search target.

"Why would they run away from home, girl?" asked her grandmother. She decided to take over the investigation, remembering the "honey versus vinegar" comparison.

Francie knew the answer but also knew she should only release so much information. The plot had been incubated ever since school started six weeks ago. Each day after school, on their way home, more aspects of the escape were brought up and voted upon. The idea probably belonged to Georgie, but it was for the benefit of Leonard.

Leonard was an abused child. His father used to beat Leonard for no apparent reason. The three friends saw but could not fathom why someone would hit their child until sound could no longer be detected from one side of the boy's head and another time when he almost died. They would measure Leonard's home life to their own. They all understood that even though times were tough and they were very poor, their families were held together with love and respect for all of the members.

"They hopped the "Nine o'clock to Mankato, Uncle George."

The plan was to leave town and start over somewhere else. The middle part was always a bit foggy; they just knew they had to get Leonard away from his father, there were no other options.

The part they knew, which contained all the bravado they needed, was the beginning, this was the part they worked out until it was flawless or as close to flawless as their teenaged inexperienced brains would allow them to plan. They would simply hop the "Nine o'clock to Mankato".

"To hop" was the verb that meant to jump on to a moving freight train thus avoiding that pesky ticket buying experience. There also was the possibility of not landing exactly inside the box car or selecting one that was already the choice of another fellow traveler or two or three and then there were the Pinkertons. The Pinkertons were the elite group of security agents paid by the Railroad Company to stop the hopping process dead, with an unspoken emphasis on dead.

They had said it enough times that it no longer sounded dangerous. They would simply hop the "Nine o'clock to Mankato" and be on their way. "The Nine o'clock to Mankato," it sounded easier and easier every time they said it and they said it hundreds of times on the way home from school in the weeks before that October night.

The train was named by the members of the village because it went through their area at nine o'clock every night and would always blow its whistle as it passed through. The whistle was the official curfew signal for the kids of Lilydale. You had to be home or at least very close to home when the locomotive signaled all the parents to make a head count.

The freight train would head south from the St. Paul yards. It may or may not have ever stopped in Mankato, but it would go through Mankato and it sure sounded romantic to the people of Lilydale and South St. Paul. Native American names always carried a certain mystic to the first and second generation Minnesotans. For all they knew, that same train was called the

Nine forty-five from Lilydale to the folks in Mankato.

"The Nine o'clock to Mankato, are they stupid?"

As a one-quarter author of the plan, Francie decided not to comment on that question but did begin to sob uncontrollably at the sound of her uncle's gruff voice.

"Dear me," her grandmother prayed out loud. "What were they thinking, Francie?"

"I don't know," she lied.

"When I get those boys..." an open-ended threat was served up by George who now remembered he had left his Dodge running in the driveway. "Mary, I've got George in my car, we will go get the boys." George was also the name of Leonard's father. It seemed that newly immigrated Europeans grasped the lifestyle of their new home with both hands and paid homage to the father of their new country by naming as many of their offspring as possible, George.

George stopped at his house to call the Railroad Company because he had one of the only telephones in the burg. "Stop that train and wait for me, I'm on my way! What? Sioux Falls? Good God! Then hold them until I get there."

All the way to South Dakota the two Georges vowed to teach all three of them the lesson of a lifetime, they even thought that their brother-in-law, Nick would be thankful for any discipline meted out to Frankie. They seemed to have forgotten all about Francie and her twenty-five percent possible guilt in the planning and her one

27

hundred percent participation in the duplicity and subterfuge after the fact.

The boys were sitting in the office of the Railroad Company when the two Georges arrived. The boys began crying as soon as they saw the two Georges. The tough men broke down and cried as they hugged the runaways. Some think Leonard's situation at home improved because of the near loss.

BLOOD IN THE SAND

"Can we go to the Bullfight? Can we go to the Bullfight?"

"No, John, not this trip." I didn't think a Bullfight was the appropriate entertainment choice for a sixteen year old.

We had decided on a family vacation to Mexico. Since the boys had never been there, it was an eye opening adventure for a sixteen year old and his eighteen year old brother. The exotic flora and fauna of a tropical destination can be mind boggling for a teenager, and the people that look so friendly but sound so confusing add to the culture shock.

We were to spend two weeks in paradise and the picture in my mind was a slow moving, sunbaked, ocean dipping, relax-fest. I knew that the boys would take it slow for the first week because the sensual overload would keep them close by until they felt like exploring more. I planned for pool time with a swim-up bar, breakfast, pool time, lunch, more pool time and dinner at some picturesque open-air dining example of Mexican coastal cuisine.

We ate breakfast at the hotel restaurant every morning and had to walk past the brightly colored placard on an easel that was in front of the concierge's office. The stylized painting showed a *torero* in mid *Veronica* with steam snorting out the nose of *El Toro*. Across the top of the picture was the phrase BULLFIGHT in English. (?) Across the bottom was the word *Miercoles,* which is Spanish for Wednesday and 4:00 which is Spanish for 4:00.

Each time we passed the ad for the controversial cultural diversion, I could hear the chanting begin: "Bullfight, Bullfight, Bullfight!"

"You know, I don't think it's what you think it is."

"Oh yeah, here El Toro!" followed by an interpretation of Sugar Ray Leonard shadow boxing down the corridor.

"Yeah, you don't get it."

"What do you have against a family outing, Jack?"

That was a vote for gore that I wasn't expecting. "Do you know what you are asking?" I asked.

"You're the one that's always talking to the boys about learning a different culture," reminded my wife.

"First of all, it's not the kind of fight you are thinking about. Besides, the tickets are eighty dollars apiece, that's a lot of money for something you guys aren't going to like. You don't know what you'll be getting into."

"Oh, we're on vacation, loosen up!"

"Matt, how do you vote?"

"I don't care, Dad. I don't feel too good; I'm going back to the room."

"Fine, I'll talk to the concierge and find out more about it." I returned at one o'clock as stated on the sign on his door. The girl at the front desk said that Arturo would be back in fifteen minutes. I sat in the chair she motioned to, it was much cooler in the little office than outside in the one o'clock Mexican heat.

Arturo entered the office. He was maybe twenty-four years old and seemed to have just bathed in Polo.

"Good afternoon, Senor. What can I do for you?"

"Some of us were thinking about the Bullfight. Can you tell you me about it, please?"

"Certainly, Senor, what a smart idea, the children will enjoy it. I can get you tickets and charge them to your room."

"Why is the Bullfight on Wednesday? Aren't they traditionally held on Sunday?"

"It's because of the cruise ships. They help pay for the Bullfight and Wednesday is cruise ship day here in Vallarta. So we have it on Wednesday."

Well, that part made sense.

"Why are the tickets so expensive, Arturo?"

"They are not so expensive, Senor. The tickets are hard to come by, especially out here in Mismaloya."

I had a feeling there were a lot of things hard to come by in Mismaloya.

"Put these tickets in the room-safe, they are valuable," I told my wife. "By the way, how is Matt? He had better be well by Wednesday or someone will have to scalp his ticket."

"I will, Dad! Bullfight, Bullfight, Bullfight!"

"No, John, that won't be necessary. And, it's not the kind of fight you think it is."

We all awoke from our various tropical dreams Wednesday morning; my wife and her shopping dreams, John and his Bullfighting dreams, Matt and his Kaopectate dreams and me and my "How the hell am I going to pay for all of this" dreams.

After pool time at the swim-up bar, breakfast, pool time, lunch and an abbreviated pool time after lunch, we got ready for our trip into town.

"Taxi to town, Senor?"

"Yes, Luis, gracias." I replied to the doorman.

Two blasts from his whistle signaled the taxi drivers waiting outside the gate that there was a fare leaving the compound. The driver in the front of the line took off and waved to his fellow drivers.

We loaded up in the cab; I sat up front with the driver and we rode out the long driveway to Highway 200. As we passed the cabbies waiting for their turn to be called, our driver tooted his horn and held out two fingers and gave them a broad stage wink.

"Where to Senor?"

"To the Bullfight, please."

"Good choice, Senor. Your sons will really like it and the senora will become very romantic, if you know what I mean. I can get you some tickets at a great price, Amigo."

"Oh, that's okay; I bought some at the hotel."

"How much did you pay?"

This was going to be that Mexican barter system in reverse. And I knew the first guy to declare didn't have a chance.

"Well, I bought them from the hotel. I paid…ah… eighty."

"Eighty pesos, good work, Senor."

"No...eighty dollars."

"Eighty dollars!? I could have got them for you much cheaper, my friend; half of that, forty dollars and I would have taken you into town for free."

All of a sudden I was the one thinking about Kaopectate. Maybe he was talking about tickets for the nose bleed section. I didn't dare tell him I paid eighty dollars each. They better have beer at this place, lots of beer.

"Oh well, maybe next time." I offered.

"What are you guys talking about up there?"

"Nothing," we said in unison.

We got to the *corrida* at ten minutes to four. The afternoon sun was beating down, unaffected by any kind of ocean breeze; even though we were only four blocks from the marina were the cruise ships moored. The parking lot was forty percent gravel and sixty percent dust. Small dust clouds formed at our feet as we walked to the round stadium. On the side of the donut shaped building, a silhouette of a bull guarded either end of the phrase *PLAZA DE TOROS.* Scalpers stood out front of the cashier window waving tickets and shouting, "Eight dollars!"

Now I really needed a beer.

Mariachi music blared over the loud speaker as we entered and I gave my gold plated tickets to the man at the gate.

"*Arriba y derecha.*" He point up and to the right. The brief time in the shade felt pretty good. I pushed the boys ahead as I brought up the rear. We moved slowly into the stucco structure. It was hot and we tried to avoid running into other hot tourists.

I had seen many pictures of *Plaza de México*, the largest bull ring in all of Mexico, located in Mexico City, a proud arena that could hold over forty-two thousand screaming fans.

When we came out of the stairway and into the sunlight, I squinted and quickly tried to do the math to determine how many *Plaza de Toros* could fit into one *Plaza de México*. Seven? Eight? I hoped it wasn't eight; I was beginning to hate that number.

We walked up about eight rows and found some space on the bench. We scooted down a little to capture any shade that might be coming at some point during the event. With the sun at our backs, we looked down into the arena. Two guys on horses circled the inside of the arena, dragging metal bed springs behind them to condition the sand.

I wondered if I should tell the boys that the word arena was Spanish for sand. They didn't look very receptive to trivia at this time. Their owl imitations lacked only the head rotation part. Mouths agape and eyes apop, they were trying to take in and process as much as they possibly could.

The arena was maybe fifty yards across, round and had a lot of pre-fight activity going on. A six foot wooden fence and a three foot wide trench separated the action of the sport from the reaction of the spectators. The first row of benches was six feet above and six feet away from the action. There were maybe twenty-five tiers of benches. The stairway allowed us to enter about ten rows up, so we were about on row eighteen. The whole stadium could hold five thousand people, maybe. Our crowd numbered eight hundred, mostly tourists from the cruise ships. You could tell which ship they were from by their white tee-shirts with the name of their ship silk screened on the front.

There was a special section down and to our right. This section sat the president of the Bullfight. The president is the official, referee and magistrate of the bullfight; his word is law.

Along with him in this section were the play-by-play announcer and the music director. Instead of the ubiquitous Mariachi band that you can find on any street corner in Mexico, the music director directed a Samsung tape recorder. Also in the special section was a beautiful young lady holding a bouquet of flowers. She must have been the president's niece; she kept hugging and kissing him. It's good to be president.

The announcer used both Spanish and English to describe the action.

When we would go to Las Vegas, we quickly realized that the waitresses that worked in the restaurants Downtown were the seasoned waitresses. The young, vital, attractive ones worked on The Strip only two and a half miles away. It became common knowledge that Downtown was where waitresses went to die.

Thus was *Plaza de Toros,* "the place where bullfighters went to die." There were eight fights scheduled for today. I picked up a list of the fights and read the small blurb about each fighter. They had very impressive resumes. Some fought in corridas that no longer existed, torn down years ago to make room for Sam's Clubs across Mexico. The fight that everyone was waiting for was number eight, a Matador named El Nino.

El Nino was the pride of the West coast. Everyone knew his name and his story. He came from a small town, too small to have a real Saint's name. It was called *Santa Nada*; that was sad. He was only fourteen years old and only four feet eight inches tall. His mom had to make his cape especially small so he wouldn't drag it in the dirt.

I didn't read this information, the guy next to me told me. His name was Miguel. He was from Mexico but lived in Los Angeles and knew everything about bullfighting. I introduced him to my family.

"Listen to him, boys. He knows what he's talking about," I instructed. "Do you guys have any questions for Miguel? Matt?"

"Miguel, where is the bathroom?"

"You mean *el bano*, amigo. It's over there behind that blanket."

Miguel continued to regale us on the history of bullfighting, as he knew it. At one point, he jumped to his feet and yelled at an old man who was carrying a five gallon bucket three rows down. The old man came up to our row.

"I will buy you guys a beer, amigo." The old man dug out three Coronas from his bucket, Miguel gave the old man a twenty dollar bill that he pealed from a large roll of twenties he pulled from his pocket. He motioned for the man to keep the change.

I began to examine Miguel a little closer now. He was a combination of both north and south of the border. He was dressed like a tourist. He wore blue shorts with a leather belt, a tee shirt with cartoon geckos copulating in fifty different positions and well broke-in huaraches. He had a big gold watch on his left wrist and a gold pinky ring on his right hand.

At ten minutes after four, the music director started the recording of "El Toro Solo" by Herb Alpert with its trumpet fanfare that everyone has heard forever. In marched all of the participants for today's event, except the bulls.

"These are the matadors for today; even those guys on the horses are called matadors. Matador means killer. The guys in gold are toreros, that means bull guys."

"Really, Miguel?"

"Oh yes, Amigos! See that guy that's next to El Nino? I saw him get gored when I was twelve; that was in 1972. I thought he died years ago. His name is Jaime Gomez; I used to have his card. They have cards like baseball cards but for bullfighters."

Having a bi-cultural guide next to us had its advantages.

Everyone exited the arena. El Toro entered from the far side. He ran directly to our side, snorted, shook his head until saliva flew in all directions then circled the arena looking for a way out. The crowd hushed except for the girl in the

37

front row who shrieked when she was hit by flying slobber.

"He's sure peessed off." Our commentary had begun.

Now the torero entered to the applause of the crowd. He walked to the middle of the ring, turned and bowed to the president. With a flourish, he spun to face the bull, he bowed to the bull.

Two men on horseback entered from the left. They each had colorful sticks with sharp points on one end. They rode up alongside the bull. Each horse wore a quilted pad under their saddle that hung low to protect them from the bull's horns. The men stuck the colorful sticks into the shoulder of the bull. Blood began to flow freely out of the wounds.

"Boy, he's peessed off now! Those sticks have razor-sharp points, like arrowheads and are connected with a swivel to the stick; the more he tries to shake them off, the more he bleeds."

"Yeew!"

"Did you say something, John? Another bano-visit, Matt?"

Two more guys in red and pink suits ran out and face the bull. The bull charged them and they poked more sticks into the bull's back and shoulders and ran away.

"Boy, he's really peessed off now!"

The torero began his dance with the bull. Who really knows what it symbolizes: male versus female, good versus evil, beauty versus grotesqueness. With each pass of the bull, the torero exhibited more bravery by exposing his back to the beast for a longer period of time with total disregard to its existence. With each pass the crowd cheered at the participants.

Like guards watching from a distance, two bullfighters stood ready to distract the bull in case it can focus enough to retaliate. Their pink capes are folded over their arms and they look like fancy waiters ready to take your order.

It was about this time when my wife leaned over and said, "You know, Jack, I have a feeling they are going to kill that bull."

"It's a blood sport! A fight to the death! I thought you understood that going into this. I kept trying to talk the guys out of it, but you were the swing vote and here we are. I spent over three hundred dollars on this and we are not leaving in the middle of the first fight. Sit back, drink a beer and enjoy the fight!"

"Boy, he's really, really peessed off now!" I think he was talking about the bull.

From a secret pocket in his cape our lead dancer pulled out a thin sword that is slightly bent at the tip. During a clumsy advance by the bull the sword is plunged into the back of the beast. Practice allowed him to find his mark; between its ribs and through its heart. The bull crumpled and collapsed into a heap before the feet of its killer.

Where a cheer and a roar usually occur, our crowd was silent with occasional gasps, some retching and three or four faintings.

Our foursome had two ashen faces, a lad running to the bano and me looking for the old man with the beer bucket.

I didn't think it could get any quieter until the horsemen returned. They hooked onto the rear legs of the once virile opponent and drug it backwards across the ring to the far side, tongue hanging out of one side of its mouth, one ear severed to be used as a trophy for the vanquisher and bloodstained back still holding the colorful sticks. The dry mouthed viewers sat quietly, trying to justify their attendance.

"They will take him out back and cut him up to give to the poor. If you want some, I know a guy who can hook you up."

"I'm cool." I felt like I was in the seventies again turning down dope.

I looked at my watch, it was still Wednesday.

"*Mas cerveza, Senor!*" the three little words a guy needs to know in Mexico.

Between bouts the grounds crew returned to condition the sand. First, two guys with wheelbarrows and shovels scooped up the blood soaked sand to haul it away, then the bed-spring guys returned to smooth out the holes.

The next two fights went on rather predictably in front of the dumbfounded crowd. Miguel would indicate which level of pissed-offness the bull was experiencing for us and our neighbors.

Suddenly, a roar and a cheer broke out in the stadium. I looked up from my beer to see Jaime Gomez flying in an arc shaped trajectory across the ring. He bounced and skidded to a stop thirty feet away. The fancy waiters sprang into action to distract the bull and two guys ran out and grabbed Jaime by his arms, dragged him to the side, dusted off his gold suit and gave him a shot of tequila.

The spectators were now united. They had a hero to worship and his name was El Toro.

"Toro, Toro, Toro!" shouted the galvanized mob, now on their feet.

The newly dusted off and fortified Jaime was pushed back to the center of the ring by the EMTs to a chorus of booing, hissing and Toro, Toro, Toro!

"I hope they let him live after this," my wife said, referring to the bull, I think. This was the hope of ninety-two percent of the assembly.

I knew it wasn't going to happen. The only thing that made the situation worse was that Jaime, being as wobbly as he was, kept missing the target area above the bull's shoulders. Four times we witnessed in horror as the point of the sword emerged from a different part of the bull's body, causing a new red fountain on the black bovine. I think the viewers were electing their own president in order to give pieces of Jaime to the bull.

A very discouraging "Ooh" escaped from our lips when the bull finally stumbled and fell. The rest was routine by now.

After the clean-up crew finished the chore of removing three loads of dark red sand and actually replacing some of it, I heard a man shouting in the stands to my right. In the middle of the ring landed a flying satchel. Everyone stared at the brown leather bag and a collective question mark rose above the crowd, much like the Bat-signal in Gotham City.

41

In five seconds our silent question was answered. An athletic looking young man jumped from the stands, over the open trench and the wooden fence and into the arena. Two members of the president's crew ran out to meet him. The young man was quite handsome and swarthy, wearing black slacks, black boots and a white long sleeved shirt; he had dark brown hair pulled back into a pony tail. He was very agitated about something and began arguing with the president's men quite vocally, pointing and stomping as he progressed.

As if in some art film, a woman appeared in front of us. She was wearing a long white flowing dress and spoke in a calm but eerie voice. She said the man in the ring was her husband; they were married on the cruise ship last week. Her husband was a professional torero in Spain, the birthplace of bullfighting. He was completely ashamed of the spectacle being displayed today in this dirty ring by these clumsy drunken has-beens; it was a complete disgrace to his art form merely to put on a show for the cruisers, what a waste of the beautiful creatures he faced every week.

The president's men tried to calm down the artisan. I'm certain they understood what he was complaining about but they also liked their jobs, working for a guy who is the president of a building.

We lasted for all of the fights on the card, even the El Nino fight. After listening to the strange interruption earlier, we were pointing out things that we thought might have been out of order. We really didn't think that El Nino should ride his skateboard in the ring and using a ladder to finish his bull might have been stretching the rules a bit.

As we left the *Plaza de Toros,* my wife looked like a candidate for a George Patton slapping, John was trying to recover from fainting three times, Matt lost eight pounds in the bano and I was trying to do the math to determine how many beers I could have bought with three hundred dollars.

In the cab:

"Where to, Senor?"

"The best steakhouse in town, amigo, I'm hungry."

"Yeeww!"

LOOKING FOR WORK-PART ONE

"If this interview doesn't work out for me, do you suppose you could check with NASA? I always wanted to be an astronaut."

"I'm sorry sir; we only search for candidates for the EPA."

Brenda tried to let me down as easily as possible. She worked for an agency that specialized in obtaining special candidates to interview for positions with government agencies. When I say "special," I mean applicants over fifty-five years old. Since I was retired, I was looking for something to do that might sound fun.

"That's okay, Brenda. The EPA sounds pretty impressive anyway."

And it did.

From what I understood, the job interview was for a lab tech to work at a real EPA laboratory with real EPA scientists on real EPA experiments.

Mwah ah ahh!

I could do this; no problem! All I would need is a size XXXL lab coat, a pocket protector and a pair of safety goggles, like the kind Gene Wilder wore in *Young Frankenstein.*

My wife, sounding a bit like Brenda from the agency, tried to ease my exuberance by suggesting, "Maybe they didn't see *Young Frankenstein*, Jack."

"They're scientists, aren't they? Geez!" I then assured her that the goggles wouldn't be a deal killer.

The interview with the EPA was in a small coastal community on the West Coast. They had a secret lab tucked away behind a well-known Marine Science Center, formerly called "The House that Keiko built." The lab and the aquarium shared the same fresh seawater supply pipeline from the Pacific Ocean.

Since the only requirement for employment was to be over fifty-five and mechanical and I set aside the "goggle perk," I felt that I had a pretty good shot.

I pulled my white hair back into a braid and I wore a red checkered shirt under my vest. I felt like Ben, Hoss and Hop Sing all rolled into one. With a neatly trimmed goatee, I was ready to kick some science ass.

I arrived early because I left early for the ninety mile trek from my house. My wife actually drove to keep me fresh for the interview. For a secret facility, they sure had a lot of directional signs marking the way. The man at the front desk immediately pointed to the restroom when he saw my wild-eyed entrance. Hey, they asked for an old guy.

I was taken for a quick tour of the facility. There were at least thirty labs stretched out inside the one story complex. They were all empty. My guide, Bill, said that at one time all of the labs were in use. He said, in the whole two acre building, only seven employees remained.

He then took me to a door that had a yellow sign with big black letters that read, DANGER.

He smiled at me and said, "This is where you will be working most of the time, Jack."

Boy, this is going to be great! I thought.

We walked down a stairway, got to the lower level, turned left and there in this dimly lit room were six large tanks. The tanks were covered with black plastic tarps. Behind each tank were three pipes. The two-inch PVC pipes were labeled with yellow tape and black letters. FRESH WATER, SEA WATER and DRAIN read the labels. The pipes had shutoff valves, pump switches and flexible plastic hoses on the ends of each.

"You will be in charge of these tanks and all of the plumbing that they need," said Bill. "Any questions about the setup down here, Jack?"

"It all looks pretty straight forward. What do you guys do here?" Now I'm curious!

"We do scientific experiments down here. These tanks hold six thousand gallons of seawater. We control the water temperature, saline content, air temperature and the amount of light the tanks are exposed to by these giant lights."

Danger! Experiments! Wow!

"What kind of experiments?"

"In these tanks we grow *Phyllospadix Scouleri.*"

Filed old spandex, what? I thought to myself, but I'm sure it was imprinted on my face.

"It's sea grass, Jack, the kind that has grown on the North Pacific Coast since the Pliocene Age. We grow it in here in these tanks and tweak with the elements and add pollutants to see how and if it is affected by the subtlest of changes. "

Grass?

"Why?"

"We do the background studying in case the EPA has to take anyone to court due to building encroachment near the grass beds. If we are already armed, we can protect the tender ecosystem more quickly."

"I get it, well that's important! What would I do here?"

"You would maintain the tanks and the pumps and plumbing."

We continued talking on our way to the interview room where I met Walter. Walter and Bill had both pulled their white hair back into a braid. They must have called my wife to see what to wear today. Walter wore a green checkered shirt under his vest touched off with brown string tie with an agate set in silver holding the braided string just under his buttoned collar. Bill wore a blue checkered shirt under his vest, sans bolo. We looked like a cloning experiment gone bad. I was a bit creeped out. I began salivating when I saw that they both had pocket protectors in the breast pocket of their vests. I scanned the room for goggles, none.

They asked me pertinent questions and I answered the best I could for twenty minutes.

"Do you have any questions, Jack?"

"Let me get this straight, we watch grass grow?"

"Or, not grow," they said in unison.

"Yeah."

In the car:

"How did it go, Jack? Do you think you got the job?"

"Gosh, I hope not."

OUR TOWN FESTIVAL AND PARADE

Last weekend our town had its annual Town Flower Festival and Parade. I can't disclose the location of my town. I'm sure you'll understand, you know, I don't want people to think I'm making fun of them and their stupid little thing.

Our town flower is the Scottish Thistle. Everything in our town has a thistle theme. The mayor starts the festivities on Thursday morning with the Thistle Cakes Breakfast. Volunteers from various service groups with the help of the Fire Department, Police Department and selected prison trustees put on an all you can eat breakfast.

Fried ham and bacon, scrambled eggs and the traditional Thistle cakes are served to everyone from eight until noon. After the breakfast the mayor along with the city council walk the two-mile trek to the top of Mount Thistle to "wake up" Scotty the festival mascot. They sing the wake up song written by the town founder Angus McAngus, "Wake up! Scotty McScott Scott, you little town mascot.."

After Scotty wakes up and puts on his special purple hat, he joins townspeople that have gathered to see the spectacle.

The townspeople will see Scotty all weekend at various venues around town. Scotty is also the grand marshal of the parade on Saturday morning. Some years Scotty is Scottie. The role is either male or female depending on who the village votes into the honorary position. It is quite an honor for any young lad or lassie to be selected. Although no money changes hands, with responsibility come benefits. The benefits in this case could be a lucrative acting contract with the local thespian society.

Perhaps you remember Jimmy Allen, the man who starred in the hemorrhoid commercial several years back. He played the guy scooting across the desert in search of relief then fell backwards into a vat of tapioca pudding. Jimmy got his start as Scotty in 1999.

With thistle fever all over town, finding room to park at the Angusville Super Mall is almost impossible. We learned early on to get our shopping done before the weekend.

This year we were inviting Andy and Randy, our grandkids, to join us to watch the parade. Andy and Randy are eight and six years old respectively and live two hours away in Mountainville. This will be their first Thistle Days Parade. We waited until we felt they were old enough to appreciate the parade and accompanying folklore. Even though the kids heard the stories for years and asked us questions every time they came to our house, they had never seen the "Waking of Scotty" or the Thistle Days Parade. Andy said he promised his teacher he would write a report and give an oral presentation. Randy was just glad to be going.

"What are they going to do with all that horse manure, Grandpa?" Randy had a million questions the night before as we ate dinner at the Thistle Dumpling.

"Just wait, you'll see," his grandmother assured him.

"Oh, Grandma!"

"I'll tell you later, Randy"

Everyone was excited at bedtime. I'm sure thistle dreams filled everyone's pillows that night.

The boys were up early Saturday morning, gobbling bowls full of Thistle-Os and asking more questions.

"Will there be those baton girls in the parade? Can I wear sun glasses? Andy hit me."

"Just wait 'til later."

The parade route was on the front page of the Angus Argus, our daily paper. The parade will start at the Angusville Mall and travel north on Scott Boulevard all the way to Thistle Downs Race Track, a distance of three miles.

We found curb space one block away from the starting point. We stretched out on the curb and eagerly awaited the parade. From our vantage spot we could see the parade forming in the parking lot of the Mall. We had arrived about a half hour early and watched the groups gather, getting ready for Showtime.

At the appointed time the parade began, led by the fire department and their five newest trucks, followed by the Chief of Police and the Mayor and city council who were wearing their round purple thistle hats.

The mounted posse riding atop their matched roans was followed by two selected prison trustees with their scoop shovels and the wagon pulled by two more. On the side of the wagon was a sign that read Angusville Prison Poop Patrol. Everyone laughed when the wagon passed. The prisoners, with their legs shackled, scurried around scooping as needed, only occasionally tripping on their chains. When they did trip, the parade watchers would roar with laughter, some would throw things at the scoopers.

Andy and Randy laughed and laughed.

"Look, Grandma! It says poop."

"Andy said poop!"

"Boys!"

Marching bands from the local high school and middle school marched side by side tooting and tweeting a marching song. The flag waving team marched and spun their large flags as they smiled broadly. The boys giggled and pointed at a small morsel that was missed by the pooper picker-uppers, white marching boots came close to stepping on it but didn't. Every near miss made the boys hold their sides. They both moaned when an antique car drove over it and flattened it to four molecules thick.

The best part of the parade for a kid was the free candy thrown out by the special interest groups that filled the space between horse groups and car clubs. The boys ran out to pick up the wrapped candy as soon as it would hit the pavement. I doubt that they were considering the three-second rule. They just wanted to get more candy. It seemed illogical but after a wave of kids ran into the street, there seemed to be more kids on the incoming wave than the outgoing wave. Great, more kids to try to find a place to sit between candy tosses.

The special interest groups fell into two types: commercial and religious commercial.

The commercial entries were pretty straight forward. You heard of their company, you understood their product and knew what was asked of you, as the observer. You had to accept the discount coupons and informational pamphlets as they are being handed out, usually as the kids were diving for candy. The paperwork was smaller than years before. A thank you was heard from Woodsy Owl.

The religious commercial entries were pretty easy to spot. A Ford F-250 four by four pickup would pull a trailer decorated with thistles and pictures of Jesus. Music broadcasted from the back of the pickup via a commercial sound mixer; the DJ wore his ball cap backwards, probably because he saw it on a news report about the music industry. The tune had a familiar ring but the words seemed quite foreign. My mind automatically went to the late sixties and some girl group that made a song about their devotion to a particular rock group. Today's lyrics were changed slightly as the people on the "float" belted out, "We love you JEE EE SUS! Oh, yes we do! We love the way you look. And miracles, too!..."

The strategy this time is to give the adults coupons for free pancake breakfast with bacon. The info is given to the kids. It is directions on how to get to VBS, Vacation Bible School. The theme of the VBS changed with the particular denominations. There was the Crusader VBS, God's Green Beret Guerillas VBS, Baby Jesus Bushwhackers VBS, Jumping Jesus Jungle Warriors VBS and Nuke 'Em Back to Bethlehem VBS. There seemed to be some prevailing theme but I couldn't figure it out.

The smallest group represented is the social interest groups: Reformed Bikers Against Old Lady Punching, Reformed Alcoholic Parents Against Child Abuse, Reformed Pedophiles Against Kitty Porn, yeah Kitty.

Andy and Randy remembered the highs and lows of the Thistle Parade on the way home. Andy had a large bag of candy, Randy's bag had a hole in the bottom. Andy got a phone number from the girl a half block down, Randy got a phone number from the guy on the Kitty Float. Andy had thirty VBS coupons, Randy lost his helium balloon as he tried to get a dumb VBS coupon.

Andy wanted pictures to go with his report on Monday. When we told him we didn't bring a camera, he was upset. I said when we got home he could Google

Angusville. Grandma said she would make him a Scotty McScott Scott suit. Randy wanted to use the phone when we got home.

We marched home, each humming a different tune.

LAST WEEKEND

"Bruno, are the lights supposed to dim when I push the shift key?"

"It's okay Boss, I fix later."

Bruno always called me Boss even though we never worked together. He was just my neighbor but had a knack for electrical things or things that made noise or seemed broken. He used to live in one of the Eastern Bloc nations where he claimed to be some kind of engineer before he came to America. Come to think of it, everyone I ever met from that region claimed to be an engineer in the "Old Country." I don't think that word translates the same as they think it does.

"If it starts to smoke again, use this, Boss." He handed me a spray bottle that resembled the one on my barbecue.

"Maybe, I'll just call my nephew; he's a computer guy for Target."

"It's okay Boss, I used to be computer engineer in Old Country. You should see my computer, it purrs like a kitchen."

Actually, I did see his computer once; it took up most of one bedroom and had moving parts and wires running from one side of the room to the other. The screen was about eight inches round. There were two keyboards; one in English and the other with Cyrillic letters on the keys. Next to the keyboards was a green rotary phone connected to a helmet, like the kind in 1960's Army helicopters, maybe our Army. On the other side of the room was the bed where four of his kids slept.

I thanked him for all of his help. On his way out, Bruno spied a broken clock-radio in the trash can outside the garage.

"May I?" he motioned to the appliance. "I can use that on my garage door opener. I used to be mechanical engineer in Old Country."

"Of course, Bruno, take it."

My wife drove up as Bruno was leaving. She waved.

"Hi, Boss Lady!"

"What was that all about?" she quizzed me.

"I had Bruno put paper in my printer."

She rolled her eyes. "I think you just have him over so you have something to write about."

"That's not true, Baby."

On a three by five card I wrote with a Sharpie, "Boss Lady" and chuckled to myself.

"You know you always make fun of that poor man and he only wants to help you."

"Oh, I do not. He said his computer purrs like a kitchen."

"Jack! And his name isn't even Bruno."

"I know, but his real name is hard to say in English."

"Boris is hard to say?"

"Well, maybe not so hard for you."

"Remember, the boys are coming for the weekend."

Andy and Randy are the grandchildren. They are eight years old and six years old respectably. They come up for the weekend whenever they can.

This Saturday, we left home early to eat breakfast at a restaurant.

"What would you like for breakfast, boys?"

"French Ghost! Grandpa, Boo La La!"

"Very nice, Andy, and you Randy?"

"I don't know. What do they have?"

"Well, it's a restaurant, Randy. They have just about everything. Do you like eggs?"

"What kind of eggs?"

"I believe they have chicken eggs."

"What kind of chickens?"

"I believe they are free range, natural, non-hormone fed Plymouth Rock egg layers that only listen to classical music."

"Really?"

"No! They are more likely to be Rhode Island Reds that live in a cage the size of your cap, that are control fed and experience a metered light and heat protocol to produce three eggs per day until they are withered away at the age of seven months."

"Really?"

"Yes."

"I'll have oatmeal, please."

After breakfast we went to play miniature golf.

"Is it called miniature golf or mini golf?"

"Good question, Randy."

"Can I have the red ball?"

"Sure, Andy, it will match your shoes."

"I'm going to practice until it's my turn. I'll go up to number twelve."

"No, Randy, you stay with us. No cheating. Watch your brother play."

Andy easily got his red ball under the big blue lion and had only ten inches to sink his putt for par. He squatted behind his ball, put his hands on either side of the bill of his ball cap and squinted at the ten inch path to the hole. He then stood over his ball, made two practice putt swings, eased into place, pulled the putter head two inches back and closed his eyes to calm himself before the tap.

"Grandma, Andy has a girlfriend!"

THWACK!!

The ball went three mini fairways south.

"Arrgh!"

"Grandma, Andy's going to hit me...OWW!"

"Andy, you have three minutes to stop hitting your brother. Don't use your...putter to hit people, that's why Mr. Wilson made five irons."

"Jack!"

"Okay, make that two minutes."

Back in the car, we relived all eighteen holes of the mini course, all the way home. It was fun.

When we got home and started getting out of the car, Bruno stopped by to invite the boys to his house. They were having a party for one or two of his sons who were the same age as Andy and Randy.

"What kind of party?"

"It's a party that celebrates a boy growing into a man when he turns seven. They serve cooked cabbage and play pin the tail on the Cossack."

"Really?"

"Be back by four o'clock, boys."

As the three of them walked down the street, I could hear,

"What kind of engineer?"

THE SOUTHWEST CHIEF

"I didn't know James Patrick O'Sullivan was Catholic!"

"Yeah, Brenda, that's why he is taking tomorrow off, to go to his nephew's baptism."

The conductor was drawing a cup of coffee from the big coffee urn in "The Lower Level Lounge and Snack Bar" of the Southwest Chief and talking to Brenda, "The Lower Level Lounge and Snack Bar" lady as we entered.

My wife Ruth and I had gone down to "The Lower Level Lounge and Snack Bar" to pick up some lunch. Brenda stopped talking to the conductor, spun around and greeted us.

"Hi, kids! Welcome to "The-Lower-Level-Lounge-and-Snack-Bar."

This was her normal greeting even though we were more than likely older than her but not by much. She would also always say, "the lower level lounge and snack bar" as if it were one word and capitalized. Brenda would make periodic announcements over the public address system telling the travelers about her lunch specials.

The announcements would always be the same but were not pre-recorded, "This is Brenda in The-Lower-Level-Lounge-and-Snack-Bar, come on down and get something good to eat," she would say with a Midwestern monotone twang. "I've got everything you need for a satisfying breakfast or lunch. I have delicious breakfast burritos and nutritious granola bars, top that off with orange juice or hot coffee or cocoa. If you want lunch items, I've got that too. I've got beef and bean burritos, deli sandwiches, cheeseburgers, hot dogs and tasty Di Giorno pizzas, you just pick out what you want and I will heat it up in my Radar Range. If you want a refreshing beverage, you can select from many cold beers, or if you are under twenty-one, try my fountain drinks or even fresh milk. You must have your ID with you to purchase any alcoholic beverages. Just come on down and see me, Brenda, at the Lower-Level-Lounge-and-Snack-Bar."

The LLL&SB was a small room on the lower level of the observation car. As you descend from the narrow U-shaped stairway, you would enter the dining area which consisted of five tables with plastic benches on either side. Beyond that was a restroom. There were two tables on the left side of an aisle way and three on the other. The right side had windows next to the three tables. The lounge/snack bar was to the right of the stairway.

Inside the snack bar were two short walls of reach-in coolers. The coolers held snack items that you would select and Brenda would heat up in one of her two microwave ovens. She would ring up these items on her cash register as the oven was humming. After the ding of the oven, she would put your items in a small box and send you on your way with a pleasant, "Thank you."

We sat at one of the tables and ate our hot dogs and drank our beer and watched the scenery go by. Another couple sat next to us prior to entering the lounge/ snack bar. They quizzed us on the quality of our choices.

"I haven't had a bad meal yet," I reported.
"Then you haven't been to the dining car."
"No, why?"

"We had breakfast there this morning and it was dreadful!"

I hadn't heard the word "dreadful" since that dowager said it in some "Our Gang Comedy" that I watched on TV when I was a kid. This dowager actually resembled the previous one.

"Oh, really?"

"I had ordered muesli with sliced fruit."

"That doesn't sound that difficult."

"They sliced the banana but they failed to peel it. I almost fainted."

"Dreadful!"

We finished our lunch and tossed our serving boxes into the recycle container next to the stairway going back up. We had to move to the side and wait for the avalanche of teenagers rolling down the stairway. The first teenager that giggled her way down the narrow stairway abruptly stopped two steps before the end thus blocking the stairway with about a dozen like-minded, like dressed, like smiley, red-cheeked, big-boned, Ohio farm grown Christians.

The smiley Christian kids got on the train at Kansas City. There were one hundred and fifty of the high school seniors with two dozen or so chaperones on their way to northern New Mexico. According to the silk screened matching yellow tee shirts, they were going to an Indian reservation to build a new church for the heathens. The helpful kids must have thought it was time to update their seven thousand-year old religion with a new and improved religion that was only two thousand years old. Hey, it worked for the Spaniards.

I could just imagine how thankful the Noble Ones would be after these white teenaged workers constructed another needless edifice they could use for storage or a place to meet while they are waiting for an ambulance to take them to the nearest clinic, one hundred eighty miles away.

For the last day and a half, the kids clogged the aisles and the entire observation deck giggling, teasing each other, posing for each other's iPhone and breaking out into spontaneous singing, accompanied with guitar, bass and tambourine. Their smiling, omnipresent, Christian parents looked on with pride from a distance, their bosoms in mid-swell. They also wore matching tee shirts.

We waited for the stairway to empty and climbed the u shaped stairway up to the observation deck. I tried to find the door at the end of the car through to students. Seven minutes later we made our way from the middle of the car to end of the car and the door out to the next car. The pneumatic door opener allowed us to escape the singing and smiling.

Our seats were two cars down. We slalomed through the first car, missing the day sleepers who were stretched out and protruding into the aisle way.

When we entered our car, there was a meeting going on. The two dozen or so chaperons were occupying the front part of our car. The leader was a man in his late thirties wearing the team tee-shirt over his orange and tan checkered shirt and red bow tie. He was addressing the twenty-three or so other parents who were standing with their backs to the front of the train.

The leader of the teen watchers was sitting in my chair. He was actually standing on his left foot; his right leg was bent at the knee and his foot was placed on my chair seat.

Grrr.

I could hear a loud creaking sound being emitted from the back of a nearby proverbial camel as the beast of burden began accumulating a load of fluffy feathers.

I found myself apologizing for returning to our own space.

"Oh, we are just holding a chaperon meeting," he cheerfully informed us.

"...mumble, mumble, our seats..."

"We'll be done in five minutes."

"My chair...your foot..."

"Oh do you want my seat?" asked the interloper.

"Do you mean our seats?"

"I can stand over here."

He moved to the other side of the aisle. He was now standing in front of a small Mexican lady who got on in St. Louis. Her eyes got big at the thought of the intrusion.

"So, any ways, when we get there, the boys will come with me and Doug Williams and the girls will go with Pamela and the other ladies to set up the campsite."

"Jack, our pillows are gone." Ruth informed me.

"They couldn't have gone too far, Baby." I looked at the two chairs behind us. Two more yellow shirted members of the "chapel chaperons" were seated in the chairs that used to support two old ladies from Baltimore on their way to Santa Fe. The man, who I recognized by his name tag as Doug Williams, second in command, was supporting the back of his head with two, very hard to come by, train pillows.

"Are those our pillows?" I asked him pointedly.

His forty-something year old eyes blinked behind his glasses. He swallowed and said, "Oh no, I brought these from Ohio." The pockets of his Dockers began emit sparks and smolder.

"Jack, those are our…"

"Let's just play nice. I know it, you know it and he knows it," I whispered. "They'll be gone tomorrow."

Grrr…*CREEAK*!

"We'll just sit here and work in our crossword magazines until their meeting is over."

"Okay."

I reached into the magazine pouch in front of my seat, it was empty.

"What the…? Have you seen my…?"

Ruth pointed to the leader across the aisle. As an impromptu clipboard holding the schedule documents was a DELL CROSSWORD PUZZLE and MORE, August edition, with ink curlicues in the corner where a pen was tested yesterday.

Grrr…SIMMER…CREEEEAK!

"Is that my magazine?" I asked the leader.

"I don't know. I don't think so."

"You do know it is not yours, don't you?"

"Oh here, I'll just hold these papers like this." He grasped his paper at the top with his hand twisted into an unnatural, uncomfortable manner, handed me my magazines and sighed.

Twenty three or so people smiled with one side of their mouth.

Grrr…SIMMER…BOIL…CREEAK!

Onto the pile of feathers that were each labeled in permanent ink: 'Teenagers', "Matching tee shirts," "Smiling," "Singing," "Tambourine rattling", "Religious arm twisting," "Superior knowledge when it came to another's culture," "Train-car high jacking," "Chair occupying", "Pillow snatching," "Pant smoldering" and

"Magazine rustling" then, floating down from the stratosphere, a feather marked "Patronizing" reached the feather pile that was held up by the sturdy ship of the desert. sweat broke out on the beast's head and a look of dread appeared on its face.

CREEEAK...CRACK...SNAP...KAPOW!!

I rose and reached for my magazine. The car was glowing crimson. I sat back into my chair. A small white dot appeared in the middle of the red curtain, covering my vision.

Like a photographic negative of the image of the oncoming black tunnel entrance, the white spot got bigger and bigger until I could see inside and then understood what I had to do. It was going to be ugly, but this had to be done and I was just the guy to do it. I told Ruth to duck and cover.

I rose to my feet, cleared my throat and as bombastically as I could, I yelled, "Hey! What the hell do you think you are doing?" Without waiting for an answer, I kept going. "You guys come in here and take over the train, clog the aisles, steal our chairs, steal our pillows, steal my crossword magazine and now you have the balls to steal the PORN that I had hidden in my crossword book. Don't you bastards have smut in Ohio? I'm sure you do! Does stolen porn get you off faster than reading your own god damn porn? Or are you just that god damn cheap? I'm going to turn my head and I expect to see my shit back on my little table when I turn back around or I'm going to the conductor and your minister!!"

I'm not a big believer in perfect timing but that day it happened. At the moment I turned to face Ruth with a wink, we plunged into the hole in the side of a mountain in Northeast New Mexico. The car went completely dark. Sixty-seven seconds later, we were back in the daylight. The chaperons were all gone. The Mexican lady across the aisle was sleeping in her chair and the ladies from Baltimore were chatting behind us.

I thought that I must have dreamt all of this until I looked down on my little table. Under our two train pillows were three different issues of Penthouse, a Playgirl and a worn out copy of Boys life.

Yeew!

- -

2012 WORDS ABOUT THE 2012 OLYMPICS

Watching the Olympics

"They arrested that old guy who rides his bike around town."

"Musty Monte?"

"Yes, Brenda at the grocery store said he was booked on sex charges."

"Honey, the guy is eighty-five years old, what was the charge, stationary rape, assault with a dead weapon? Are sure she didn't say six charges?"

"Come to think about, it could have been six. Brenda wears those big braces on her teeth and she is very hard to understand and they were calling for a clean-up on aisle eight at the same time."

"Is that the girl whose dad made her braces at work?"

"Yes, she said he is a welder and works with stainless tubing."

"We have got to move out of this town and the sooner the better."

"Everyone we know lives here."

"Bingo!"

My wife was right but so was I. Our town is more than likely the same as any other town on the planet with the same amount of odd characters per capita. It just happens we know most of these odd characters. We don't seek them out but if I were paranoid, I might think they sought us out.

There was the lady who stopped what she was doing, spun around from her work, pointed at my wife as she was standing in line and yelled out that she liked the fact that Ruth has a small cute nose and stated that she wished she could take it home with her. Aside from being embarrassed, Ruth has refused to enter the Post Office since.

The guy that pumps gas down the street refers to himself in the third person and the real weird part is his name is George Washington. "Can George Washington help you?" By the time I figure out what he is really asking me, the guy behind me is laying on his horn. "Hey, George Washington is working here as fast as he can, Mac! If you don't calm down right now, George Washington is going to kick your cracker ass."

I could go on but if I tell too much, you would know where I live.

Last week I was watching the Opening Ceremonies for the Olympics. After I got over the day dreaming episode I always experience every four years about winning a Gold Medal for crossword solving, I sat in my chair and took in all that I could.

The first week showed few surprises. The French surrendered to the Germans in three sports. China dominated all factory sports and the products will be available at Wal-Mart next week. USA basketball players tweeted everyone on the planet six times over.

The rest of the Olympics went pretty much like all the previous Olympics. Some athletes broke records, some let down their fans and their country, some went home victorious, and some didn't make it home at all. We began to realize that the sports power behind the former Soviet Union came from the outlying now separate states, Catch-it-Stan and You-betcha-Stan.

I started thinking about the thousands of participants who come from thousands of towns around the world. I began doing the math in my head; our earth must contain millions of odd characters, and what about places that are already messed up to begin with? That might answer a lot of questions about world politics, these world leaders that are creating so much concern around the world must come from some really messed up neighborhoods.

That little nut from Iran must have been from a really crazy neighborhood to be elected Mayor of Tehran and then President. If he is the cream of the crop, I can just imagine what their postal workers must be like; they probably go home with a pocket full of actual cute body parts that they actually remove from people waiting to mail their birthday cards.

We had a phrase in the old days that the first liar never has a chance. Can you picture a therapy group where everyone is trying to get the others to hear their story about their terrible childhood? You just got done crying your way through a rendition of how your dad didn't get home until six o'clock, and you felt neglected because you were watching TV by yourself for a half an hour while your mom made dinner. Everyone in the group was getting teary eyed and in walks Kim Jong-un. Shit! Time to go home!

I guess I'll reconsider my idea about moving out of my nutty burg. I already know the crazies in my town and by comparison there are screwier individuals that I can see right on TV. If these folks are the people they are proud enough to show to the world, what do the "local locos" do that other villagers want to hide from the public?

So I'll just sit back, watch the Olympics and work my crosswords. I do have a hard time convincing my wife that during the original games in Greece, they did their crosswords in the nude.

A Midsummer Olympic Night's Dream

I was watching the Asian women play Table Tennis, I found myself fantasizing... I would like to watch them butter toast.

Another thing I noticed while watching the women's Table Tennis, the players have to shag their own errant balls. In Lawn Tennis, there are eight twelve year old kids who run down, bring back and toss to the players all of the out of bounds attempts. In Lawn Tennis, the player wears the latest designer fashions; in Table Tennis, the Asian girl was wearing a Tee-shirt with one of those stickers stuck to the front of her shirt that says "HELLO, my game is PING PONG."

I was watching soccer today, or as we call it, soccer. I understand the difference between football, *futball* and soccer. I know that England had *football* since the early fifteenth century.

As England colonized the world, it introduced football as an organized pastime activity. It wore out the colonist so that insurrection was out of the question. The Spaniards, on the other hand, just sent their colonists to church, or else.

The soccer game I was watching was between a team from Asia and a team from Africa. I saw a collision between two opposing players. They struck each other head on with such force that they ended up ten feet from each other. On to the pitch ran their respective medical people and coaches.

The Asian healthcare worker attended to the writhing player by crouching over him; her assistant held a small bronze burner full of a medicinal smudge that poured out smoke over the head of the player. The first worker administered one well-placed needle into the neck of the striker. At the count of four, the needle was removed; the player sat up, shook his head, jumped to his feet and rejoined his team.

The other casualty, also writhing, was attended to by his coach and a tall, thin bald man wearing a flowing yellow kaftan. He sat cross legged next to the patient. From a concealed pocket, he produced a small skull cap shaped wooden bowl. He shook the bowl and emptied the contents onto a small piece of leather that he had spread out on the ground. Bone fragments landed in a peculiar pattern. He stirred them with his long forefinger, looked up to the coach and sadly shook his head. The coach motioned to the sidelines. Two men ran in with a stretcher and removed the player.

I was watching the Olympics last night; the beach volleyball contest was a bit confusing. If they are playing at nine thirty at night, local time, why do the players wear sun glasses? I also noticed that the uniforms varied from very small bikinis like the Brazilian team wore to long sleeved shirts which were sported by the Polish team. The women's fashions were even more confusing. I guess the type of uniform has a lot to do with the weather at the beach to which one normally plays or the Poles just need the long sleeves to get their entire name on the back of their jersey.

I also noticed that after each point, the beach volleyball women would embrace each other to celebrate their achievement. This seemed to become a contest within a contest, when in turn the hugging team would take a bit longer than their opponents, then the rubbing of chest parts began and then there was the slap on the backside. I went outside to work in the garage. When I told my wife, Ruth, she said that she saw a girl on the water polo team pull down the top of an opponent's swim suit. Why didn't she wake me up?

I heard there was an IOC investigation today. The International Olympic Committee is looking into the rumor that the Field Hockey player from India, Cindy Johnson, is playing under an assumed name.

Our women's soccer team jerseys look like that "Where's Waldo?" guy's shirt.

Our favorite breakfast restaurant now serves Freedom Muffins instead of English Muffins. Now I think I would like to see one of those Asian girls butter my Freedom Muffins.

Olympics, an Overview

"Jack, why are the Beach Volleyball women wearing wrist watches?"

"So they can tell how long people are going to care about their so-called sport?"

"Yeah, maybe."

"Maybe they should have used their watch money to buy some sun screen, when they stand next to each other, they look like John Wayne's saddle bags in True Grit."

"That's for sure."

…later…

"WEEVIL, WEEVIL HRAUTCK CHOO!"

"What are you watching now?"

"Men's Wrestling: Armenia versus Thailand."

"Who is singing?"

"It's hard to tell."

You know, I always look forward to the Olympics, but about in the middle of the second week, Ruth, my wife, and I are experiencing Olympic overload. I wake up at four o'clock and follow the games on my computer and on TV. I watch three events at once. When Ruth gets up, I report to her everything I have witnessed. If need be, I show her the recording.

At about eleven o'clock, I have a small rant attack. The later in the Olympic season, the accumulation of angst builds up faster than at the beginning. I begin to question the things that I probably would have let slide earlier.

How can the commentator tell one more sad story about an athlete or a member of his or her family or someone in his or her town or country and how winning a gold medal at the Olympics will fix them right up?

How can the citizens of our country act like we are proud of our newest generation of the Dream Team while they pull down the pants of countries like Nigeria on the court and act as though the people at home condone this bullying behavior as we ask our congress to pass anti-bullying legislation?

How can the network broadcast every chance to play our National Anthem yet never play the patriotic songs for countries that are not our friends?

How can we believe our TV commercials about how our corporate sponsor/partner for our Olympians this year was last year's villain who help lay waste to thousands of miles of delicate coastal beaches and estuaries in our country? Remember? Remember?

How can we not get excited about the young girl from Yemen, who was the first female in her country to go to the Olympics? She did not win a medal but she broke barriers that millions in her country and her country's history could not enjoy. Where was the commentator that day?

As the games come to an end, we think about the two plus weeks when we all stopped our seeking of differences and found the similarities in us all and rooted for our favorite athletes. We hopefully saw enough amateur sports drama to last the two years we must wait until the winter games in Sochi.

Here's to you, Zeus, thanks for inspiring us. I can sleep in now.

BAR HOPPING IN WISCONSIN

"Our new Big Boy 35,000.2 Super Tough Guy, one ton, Diesel dually, 4-WD, Pickup is now chock-full of everything todays rancher needs, built right in. These pickups are loaded with the stuff it takes to make it out there:

Six eight-ply Super Tuff 360, puncture proof, off-road work boots

200 gallon standard fuel tank

Tinted windows and glass

Knotty Pine wood grain interior, hand carved from rough-cut four by four lumber

Military grade GPS with real-time satellite imaging and cloaking

Built-in 15kw generator

On-board air compressor with 50 gallon holding tank for air-brakes and such

Double welded, powder coated tie-downs

Built-in Winchester .30-30 lever-action rifle*

Pick one up today!

*Firearms are only available in Wyoming and Arizona."

I saw that ad in my Sunday supplement. Man, I wish I could write like that. Actually, I wish I could read that out loud without giggling. I tried using my best Sam Elliott voice but since I quit smoking again over seven years ago, I sounded more like Chris Elliott.

You know it's hard to believe but they're really brothers. I met them both in a bar in Wisconsin; they were

- -

shooting some cheese commercial together. The slogan was "We are nerds for curds!"

Boy, did they have some goofy stories about the old days.

That's not my most outrageous Wisconsin bar story, not by far.

I always have the same requirements when it concerns a good watering hole:

A nice quiet place to have a beer and converse with my company, who is usually my wife, Ruth.

Seventies rock, sixties rock and roll, fifties country or silence

An informative bartender but not too informative

Interesting clientage but not too interesting

Clean environment but not too clean

One day we were seated in another bar in the Badger State, nursing our beer so we wouldn't have to leave, just enjoying the surroundings. There was a man next to me to my right, three stools down. He appeared to be a regular guy, maybe a regular customer. Next to him sat a lady in her fifties. He was talking to the bartender in low tones. She must have been there for some time. Some people speak louder after a few beers. She was slurring as loud as she could.

"You're an Indian, aren't you?" she stage whispered to the man next to her, leaning in to hear his answer. She was now holding her head with her right hand as she propped it up using her elbow on the bar as a base.

"Yes, I am," the man replied.

"You know...I think I must have some Indian blood in me because I have a...I have a problem with alcohol.

You know...you know...how you guys have a problem with alcohol?"

My wife, the bartender, the man and I all rolled our eyes in unison upon hearing that.

Wow!

"That's why I think I might be part Indian because I can't stop drinking. I like my alcohol. So should I do something special?"

"Quit drinking, ma'am," the man said softly.

"Well, I never! You don't have to get uppity, boy."

The hair stood up on at least three necks.

"I mean...I'm sorry...I get carried away. Let me buy you a drink, friend," she tried to quiet herself.

"It's okay, I'm fine, thank you, ma'am. I'm used to it."

"No, really...I'm sorry. Bartender, what is he drinking? I want to buy him another drink!"

"He's drinking an iced tea, ma'am."

"Iced tea? What's he doing in a bar if he's only drinking iced tea?"

"He's my brother. He came in to tell me our father died last night."

"Was it alcohol related?"

"Yes, ma'am," explained the bartender. "He was struck by a drunken driver on his way home from work last night. He was a surgeon at the children's hospital. No one in our family drinks. You were right, lady, we've got a problem with alcohol; we don't like it. Here's your tab, ma'am. I've already called you a taxi."

If this wasn't so far from home, I know I would have a new favorite bar. I like those guys.

But my favorite place wasn't even a bar. It was a store, a store devoted to all the things you can do while drinking beer, except driving a school bus. It was a store based on the Bass Pro format. It was next to the Leinenkugel Brewery. It was the Leinies Store.

Leinies was the nickname of a local favorite beer. They built a store to highlight products with the Leinie logo. You could also purchase beer at the store, to drink there or to go.

Leinies must be the beer devoted to the sporting life because everything sporting had the Leinie Logo: camping gear, tennis balls, outdoor wear, shirts, shoes, caps, jackets, canoes, tents, barbecue equipment, golf clubs, jai alai, and yacht racing gear.

The people of Wisconsin love their beer and proudly wear their Leinie-Wear where ever they go. I saw a photograph of a couple getting married in Leinie-Wear; the minister was wearing a Leinie cap shaped like a Walleye.

I saw people at the Piggly Wiggly wearing Leinie swimsuits getting ready to go to the lake.

The one person I saw who wasn't wearing Leinie-Wear was a man in uniform. He was, however, buying the famous beer at the Piggly Wiggly. He had a grocery cart full of cans and another cart full of ice. He struggled with his load and I asked if I could help him. He declined my offer and struggled all the way to his van where the entire scout troop was waiting, singing camp songs.

Hmmm

APARTMENT 3G

"Ah, damn it, Honey; I spilled gravy on my diet pills."

"What?"

THWUP, THWUP, THWUP!

"Never mind, I just cleaned them up."

"I received a thanks-but-no-thanks letter from the employment department of the state today."

"Really? That's too bad," my wife, Ruth, always knows when a kind word helps.

"Well, it was a bit embarrassing. I must have misread the ad because the letter they sent me kept repeating that the job was a boil-er inspector, boiler inspector. That was a bit different than I prepared my resume to reflect."

"EWWW!"

"That's okay; they know me by name at the state by now. Remember the time they had the governor send me a personalized letter to thank me for applying for the position of State Alchemist? It was very nice of him to take the time to write that letter. He tried to convince me that there wasn't such a job. I read about it on the internet. They have a secret laboratory in the mountains high above Capitol City where the state alchemist works, turning lead into gold."

"Jack, you've got to stay off those weird sites, you'll pick up some kind of virus that I won't be able to get off your computer. Remember that time you had to have me help you remove those pictures of sumo wrestlers' backsides?"

"When it said Moon Shots, I thought it meant *the* Moon."

- -

"That's my point, you fall for all of those internet tricks."

"I still think there is a secret lab inside hidden caves in the mountains."

"Well, you keep trying, Jack."

Sometimes I think she just wants me to find a part time job in order to get me out of the house. She claims I still bark orders in my sleep in the same salty way I used to back when I was working. I don't know about that, but some mornings I awake completely refreshed but my voice is gone for a few hours.

We were discussing the internet and e-mails when she stopped talking. I spun around to see what she wasn't saying. Her eyes got big and she did that same sweeping thing with her eyes that she does when my zipper is down in public. I instinctively looked down, but then I realized that her eyes were sweeping side to side not the customary up to down. I followed the sweep to look outside our patio door. There was a lad standing in our back yard.

"Don't scare him, Jack," she whispered, as though he were a lost fawn.

We live in a modest apartment complex on the noisy side of a quiet suburb in the Pacific Northwest. I have unofficially renamed our street Runway Avenue. People who have decided they have had all the fun they can take in our town use Runway Avenue to accelerate to freeway speed before they enter the Interstate, two miles away.

From our place, one could see the black marks on the street left by the burning tires of the departing drivers. From just before they reach our place until the Interstate freeway, the drivers have a straight shot where they will only encounter four traffic lights, three churches, two schools and a shopping center.

We lived here long enough that my wife could tell just by sound how many people were in an ambulance as it screamed passed our place on its way to the village triage center just west of here.

We considered our backyard to be all of the area from the sides of our apartment extended out toward the runway. Our backyard contained a tall pine tree, a small shrub, a plant that used to be a shrub but was now a tall leafy something and a tree that has more dead limbs than live leaves. The foliage cuts down some of the traffic noise and filters most of the burning rubber smell and affords some privacy. Well, it did offer some privacy until the yard crew trimmed enough leaves so that Ruth told me that I have to wear pants now, all day.

Behind the shrub/tree stood a smallish boy with reddish brown hair; he had enough brown hair mixed in to prevent a daily ass kicking at school, I hope. I stood up, opened the patio door, walked onto the deck, tilted my head in an inquisitive way and waved at the boy. He was frozen in place. Ruth was right again with her silent caution.

I approached the rail of the deck and said, "Hello? Are you okay?"

He swallowed, nodded his head and emitted a near silent, "Yes."

"Do you live nearby?" I quizzed.

"Yes, we just moved in to apartment 3-G, we are your new neighbors. My name is Bobby. I'm not doing drugs in your backyard."

"What?"

- -

Not knowing which declaration I was questioning, he chose to repeat the last two statements. "My name is Bobby and I'm not doing drugs in your backyard."

"Bobby, I never thought that you would be doing drugs in my backyard." I had to raise my voice to carry over the siren of the ambulance inbound from somewhere on our two mile runway. I glanced back to Ruth; she put two fingers on her left sleeve indicating that two people were on their way to the hospital; she twisted her wrist left to right which means one in serious condition and one with just scrapes and bruises.

"Well, I'm not doing drugs in your backyard, sir."

I never heard so much talk about drugs since sixth grade. We just got scared straight in fifth grade over blasting caps, whatever they were.

"Bobby, my name is Jack and I can tell you are not doing drugs in my backyard. How old are you?"

"Fourteen and..."

"I know, and you're not doing drugs in my backyard. It's okay, relax." He might have been fourteen, but he was the size of a ten year old. I guess the ass-kickings are back on the schedule. "I'll tell you what, Bobby, I sometimes act fourteen so I won't do drugs in your backyard. Truce?"

"Okay."

I looked up to watch a Home Depot semi leave the tarmac down by the Dairy Queen and begin his final checklist for takeoff to Denver. When I looked back down, Bobby was gone, presumably not doing drugs in someone else's backyard.

I started a mental list of all the people that paraded through Apartment 3-G.

Before the non-drug-taking Bobby and his family arrived, there was the couple from Idaho or someplace.

He was training to be a manager at a chain store. She got my attention by being the only person to drop the f-bomb and the n-word together in the first sentence uttered and that includes thirty five years working with construction workers. Her second sentence informed me that she was a substitute preschool teacher.

Before the gutter-mouth, the place was empty for almost four months while it aired out from the bartender and her two young boys. The boys were seven and eight. She had a dog and a cat that took turns marking their territory in the front room. The property manager had to dig down through the carpet and passed the sub-floor to remove enough "stained" flooring to freshen the smell in there.

Before the always relieved pets, four guys lived there, three inside and one in the garage; they were always tinkering on cars. Later we found out the cars belonged to other people who didn't know they were even missing. At least the guys were very quiet.

Once, two guys began making beer in the garage next door. They moved out and now own a brew pub downtown.

I always wondered why the place was as busy as a bus terminal. Maybe it was the sirens, maybe the proximity to the hidden caves used by the state alchemist.

GHOST WRITING

"He killed me! He kiiillled me!" the eerie moan moved through the rooms of the all but empty manor.

When the sound entered the candle-lit study, it passed directly through the bodies of the participants of the séance. It started at Madame Zelda, the Gypsy Medium, traveling through their clasped hands, but being felt deep inside their bodies like blast from the ship's horn that they all experienced that morning when they landed at Constantinople.

A lightning flash lit up the room as though it were mid-day and not mid-night. They all saw the message written with blood on the large mirror hanging on the study wall: HE KILLED ME. Lady Penelope shrieked. She used her hands and handkerchief to try to stop the scream from exiting her lips; she slumped from her chair and fell to the ground.

HE KILLED ME....

Now to me, that was classic ghost writing, you know, the kind we saw in movies like *Abbot and Costello meet somebody scary*. Then I saw an ad on Craig's List. I used to read the job ads, but I saw an ad in the personals column that intrigued me. The way I understood it, I wouldn't even have to get naked.

"Ghost Writer needed", read the headline. "For 411, call 5 fifty-five 1 twenty-one 2."

Now I'm hooked because I didn't understand any of that.

"Ruth, can you translate this for me, please?" Whenever I need help figuring what's what in today's society, I call for my wife, Ruth. She always knows what's happening; I don't know how she knows this stuff because she is usually right next to me all day long. I think she just pays attention better than I do.

"You know, those Craig's list ads can be unreliable, and they always want you to get naked."

"No, this one is different, I think, look."

"According to this ad, someone want's a ghost writer and to get more information, you have to call, 555-1212"

"Really? How do you know all of this stuff?"

"I read."

"Ohhh."

I called the number. I spoke to a girl named Bhrehnndah, she spelled it for me.

"What is it you need written?" I asked.

"Oh! My God! Are you a writer? With words and all?"

"Words and some punctuation."

"Really? Wow! I got punctuated when I got my piercings."

"?"

"Here's what I need. I was thinking about a story. About a girl who saves the world by texting. She could be like called Text Girl or 4G Girl and have a BFF named Bhrehnndah. Do you think you can do it?"

"Hmmm. You've got a lot of blanks to fill in there."

"Yeah, isn't it cool?"

"I'll get back to you. You keep working on building your characters and maybe add to the plot a little bit. I'll call you back in a couple of weeks, Bhrehnndah."

"I will, Jack. I'm also going to take a class in meditation."

"?"

"I told you, Jack," reminded my wife.

The following week:

There was a woman who needed a ghost writer to put down on paper the true story of her friend who was sexually abused as a child, then as a teen and even more as a young adult. She wanted it put into a three act dramatic-musical play.

She wanted to meet to go over the details. I carefully backed out of this one, telling her that I was more accustomed to writing about characters that are up-beat, not beat up; besides, that situation had getting naked written all over it.

One day Ruth came home from the grocery store. I watched as she struggled to carry in our week's larder. As she set the load on the kitchen counter, I asked if she needed a hand.

"No, I've got it now, thanks anyway."

"No problem."

"I was talking to my friend, the checker at the store—"

"The girl with the homemade braces on her teeth?"

"She can't help it; she has to wear them. Her dad made them for her at work. She's proud of her father and he loves her. What I'm trying to tell you is that her mother is retiring from her job at the hospital."

"Doesn't she work in the baby department?"

"Yes, she's the one that takes the pictures of the newborns, they will be looking for someone to replace her."

"I could do that!"

"That's what I was thinking."

"Yeah, I could start there and work my way up."

"To what? You can't become a doctor. You don't work your way up in the medical profession like you can in the construction industry."

"I bet I could, but that's not the job I was thinking of. I want to work my way up to Baby Namer."

"There is no such job, Jack, get serious. People name their own babies."

"People name their own babies based on emotion, like your friend wearing the homemade braces on her teeth. She wears them because she loves her father, but real braces would improve her smile faster with fewer weird reactions. I would name them based on logic, you know, the Indian way. It would be the perfect blend of observation, imagination and lexicography."

"The job is for a photographer, Jack."

"First Poland, Baby, first Poland. Hmmm."

Ruth went back to work in the kitchen.

Yep, everybody needs their own Poland. I could see this baby picture gig as a stepping stone to Baby Namer or as I would call it NOMENSCHICKER or giver of names. The previous is a good example of a good Namesmith.

I don't know about you, but I have heard a lot of names that really sound ridiculously homemade. I don't think there is a big mystery that we hear these names on the news. Imagine the angst these young people carry with them as a young boy named "Otto 'Buster' VanBuster", arrested for operating a chop shop in the chop shop district of downtown or the girl named "E.Z. McLegspread" who was arrested in the brothel district last night.

People should also stay away from trying to capture the warmth they feel for their own current singing idol or movie star. I remember back in third grade when a new student arrived in the middle of the year. His name was Rudy Vallee Guillespie. Since the obvious reference was before our time, maybe influenced by a grandmother, we jumped on the name we recognized by greeting him with our hands in front of us, fingers pointed up and wiggling and using our best imitation of a speaker box in the doctor's lounge we would say, "*Ksssht...*Dr. Guillespie to O.R., please! *Ksssht!*"

Kids do say the darnedest things.

You can bet if a girl is named Little Debbie, her mom is more than likely overweight.

Creative spelling would also be bypassed; remember Bhrehnndah?

People should also stay away from those crazy names that celebrities give to their spawn. You would think their names should be easier to pronounce than all other names because eventually a junior college graduate will have to read them during roll call at a rehab clinic.

My new position would afford me a sneak peek at the baby's photo. This would help establish possible physical characteristics that might be an obvious give away to what the child should be named.

This will help the child in school by putting out there the easy "put down" before the other kids can figure it out, thus nullifying their efforts of offending, since most bullies aren't very inventive or able to get beyond the obvious. If you met someone named "Hooknose Peterson," as a bully, you really can't add much more to that. Thus maybe after a few generations of logical naming, bullies might be out of a job. Wouldn't that be nice?

It would also cut down on those embarrassing moments when you can't recall someone's name, but by just looking at them, you can use logic to come up with it.

When that young woman greets you by name, you can survey her face; notice the silvery beads of spittle on the corner of her mouth and respond with confidence, "Bubbles! I haven't seen you forever!"

How easy is it to remember the muscle-bound he-man when his name is Chester? Or a top-heavy woman named Bobbie?

Observation, imagination and lexicography have kept naming simple for thousands of years. Let's get back to basics which actually would be the perfect job for a Ghost Writer/Photographer.

- -

MY TRIP DOWNTOWN

WARNING: The following story contains graphic accounts and may not be suitable for some readers.

I bruised my wiener last week.

I know, I know, I don't usually write so crudely, but I did warn you. That's what the warning was all about.

Now it's out-of-the-way, I better get on with my story.

I never believed my kids when they said that they were minding their own business and then something inexplicable happened. I guess I should have been more believing as a parent.

I was walking down the street, minding my own business. That does come out easily.

I was meeting my friend for coffee at a trendy coffee selling place just north of downtown. I needed to cross the street, but since I had a hard time checking both directions of oncoming traffic due to parked cars, I had to commit and walk halfway across the street. I was standing in the turn only lane, waiting for the northbound traffic to slow down and a helpful motorist stopped to let me finish crossing the street.

I got safely to the other side and began slowing down because I never want to be seen running, I guess it is an acting cool thing or that the sight of a XXXL, fifty-nine year old running may scare some people.

I had my feet in braking mode, but the rest of me hadn't got the message yet. Shuffling to slow down, my left foot found a segment of concrete that was an inch taller than the one before it. My left foot stopped immediately, the rest of me, not so much.

I've fallen down before, I am no stranger to gravity, but this time was different.

Usually, as I float to the earth's surface, there seems to be plenty of time to re-adjust position, check my watch for accuracy, smooth out any wrinkles in my shirt and respond to those little naked angels as they fly by asking, "Hey Jack, how's it hanging?"

"Great, guys, but I'll get back to you in a little bit."

"Have a nice trip!"

"Yeah, see you next fall!"

I would achieve touch-down, complete two or three push-ups, since I'm down there, and spring to my feet, dusting my hands together. I then look to that hard to please Russian judge with a wink, for a perfect ten.

This time, however, since my knees were locked and feet were stopped dead, I tipped over much like a refrigerator-sized domino. My hands hung helplessly at my sides, they were not needed in this landing effort. The Russian judge was not looking.

Much like Navin Johnson, I was saved by the bill of my cap. I landed completely flat and in unison with all my parts landing at once; cap bill, chin, shoulders, thighs and knees. The compression of my cap bill being pushed against my cranium and then released, shot my cap four feet ahead of me, I arched my back to avoid further damage, brought my hands forward and began to run a complete parts check, looking for holes or moisture. I found my glasses and ball cap and re-applied both.

I was trying to remember how many teeth I normally sport. I began counting, using my tongue as a pointer, I got to three and discovered a sizeable hole in that part of the inside of my mouth just below my lower lip. I don't really know the name of this part of my body. It seems my teeth were pushed into the inside of my lower lip.

Before I could right myself, two people stopped to assist me. This both impressed me and embarrassed me.

An old guy on a shiny red Harley pulled up onto the curb, stopped, dismounted and was at my side in seconds. A soccer-mom jumped out of her SUV that she parked around the corner. They both began to debrief me, but not the way you are thinking.

One asked me if I was okay and the other asked if I needed help. Even in my impressed/embarrassed, groggy state, I realized that to satisfy both of them I had to give an affirmative and a negative response at the same time.

I continued my dental inventory as quickly as possible so that if I would open my mouth I wouldn't have to worry about picking teeth up off the ground.

The shiny red Harley that was hastily parked on the corner of the sidewalk began to list. When it got to forty-five degrees, I realized that I was talking to the old guy, "Hey, Buddy, your bike!" It fell completely over. The biker righted it and set the kickstand.

"It's my street bike, don't worry about it! Are you okay?"

I looked at him, astonished that I could talk. I closed my mouth and continued my inventory. I thought that the adrenaline was affecting my ability to count.

The soccer-mom continued to quiz me, "Do you need help?" she was holding her cell phone for me to see. I was certain that she had already punched 9-1- and was waiting for my reply to determine if the other "1" was necessary.

"I think I'm okay," I reported to my new friends. "Am I bleeding?"

"No, I don't see any blood," said the biker.

Now I was checking out the rest of my body. My hands were clean; I realized they didn't help break my fall. Thanks, hands! I used my clean hands to pat myself down, looking for rips or tears in my surface; I determined that I must still be in one piece.

Confused but trying not to act confused, I declared that I was not hurt and thanked both of my new friends.

"Okay, Man!" said the biker. "Don't worry, that's why Jesus put me here."

"?"

The lady waved her cell phone one more time, wearing a concerned look on her face but still standing close to her SUV, she stayed in the street.

"I am fine," I insisted. "Thank you!"

To prove I was not harmed, I tried to inject some humor. The only thing I could think of was to say, "Thursday!" Since it was Monday, the woman clutched her phone close to her breast area, arched her eyebrows and ran around to her SUV. She sped away before I could explain that it was an old boxing joke, but I thanked her again as she left.

Feeling like an old stumblebum, I walk down the street to meet my friend for coffee, I opted for ice water and a napkin. While I talked with my friend, I would stop every couple of minutes to check for blood or teeth ready to fall out.

An hour later, I rose from my chair and traveled back to my car, a little more wobbly than normal and a lot more humble.

For those of you waiting for the salacious part of the story; the next morning I woke partly bruised on part of my lower parts. With the use of three mirrors, I was able to detect the pain I was experiencing was caused by a bruise. I had to convince my wife I did have my pants on at the time of my fall. I also realized how lucky I was that I didn't feel this pain at the time I got up from the ground at the coffee shop.

I could just see myself in a groggy, foggy state counting my teeth then feeling pain and asking the helpful lady if she thought I was bruised. She would have punched in the final "1" and locked herself in her SUV.

The second and third days are always the worst in these "body to ground" collisions; stiff and sore muscles and sore and unstiff other parts take some getting used to.

There is an inability to pronounce certain words due to your fat lip and tender mouth: Walla Walla, Predicament and Garbage Disposal to mention a few.

There were some important things I learned during my recovery week: Band-Aids don't stick very well to the inside of your mouth, time does heal wounds, not everyone wants to see all of your bruises and when you look like a drunken bum people will stop to help you or call the cops or take your picture, as needed.

Today, I learned if you warn someone not to look, they will look anyway, right?

NEIGHBORHOOD WILDLIFE

Ruth slammed on the brakes. The car stopped almost immediately because we had just taken off from the curb in front of our apartment. She rolled down her window and craned her neck through the hole.

"HEY!" she shouted out the window.

I never heard her raise her voice in the eight years we were together. It was very impressive. Just in case, I sat at attention in the passenger's seat and did a quick inventory around me to see if maybe I forgot something.

"HEY, I'M TALKING TO YOU!" as she backed up the car.

I'm off the hook. She's talking to someone who is not within my scope of vision and she is serious.

"That is a wild animal! That is not a cat! Do not pet that animal! Back away and go home now!" Ruth's voice was direct and forceful.

I kind of liked it. I mean it gave her an authoritative platform I had never seen before. Now I had to figure out what was going on.

She backed up a little more and I could see what she saw. As we left our house, a mother raccoon and her two kits ran onto our front porch, closely followed by two neighbor kids. "Look, Kitty!"

The neighbor kids were two of the many nameless kids who grow wild in our neighborhood. They were eight to ten years old and weighed in at maybe forty pounds each. We always see them hanging out with other seemingly unattended children from the area.

We had seen them taking turns lying on the speed bump near their apartment while the others would sit on the curb and make the "*DING DING, DING DING*" sound

95

as cars would drive past the nearly invisible kids. I have also seen one of these kids lying on a skateboard using her hands to propel her across the parking lot. It brought back memories of Gidget and Moondoggie paddling out to catch a big wave.

The raccoon mother would bring her kits down to the suburban territory to teach them how to find food in every cat food dish in the entire town. Unlike her human counterpart, she would know at all times where her young were and challenged anything that she would deem a danger to her babies.

"They are not cats!" warned Ruth, as the protective mother stood on her back legs. The mother hissed and puffed up to help conceal her young who were trying to catch a peek at the approaching play companions.

"No, don't stop," I whispered, as I tried to calculate how many Band-Aids it would take to complete the recovery process and then multiply that number by two. I would write this number on a 3X5 card and hand it to the pharmacist at the Piggly Wiggly Store along with a five dollar bill to cover my bet.

"Sometimes it's better to not interfere; Baby, besides those kids can't really hurt the Raccoons."

"Grrr!"

OUR LITTLE FRIENDS

PECK...PECK...SPLASH!
PECK...PECK...SPLASH!
"It's six o'clock, Baby."
"Are they here?" asked my wife, Ruth.
"Yup. Right on time." Those guys had perfect timing. I don't know what kind of birds they are. There are four of them, they are black, brown and white, about the size of a golf ball and if they live long enough, they could be called Snow Birds.

For the last week or so, they have arrived on our back deck at six o'clock, drank water and bathed in the pie pan that Ruth has provided for them. It is fun to watch the little puff balls cavorting in the pie pan.

One of them always takes a turn as sentry, waiting on the branch of the tree next to the deck that has more dead limbs than live leaves. His head swivels about, looking for danger. If he knew that Ruth was already guarding them, he could join his little buddies.

The caution is there because of the stupid neighbor's stupid cat. This cat is a smarmy black and orange, grease spotted calico that our new neighbors brought with them from Hell. Since outdoor cats are not allowed where we live, the neighbors ignore their cat all day until they want it to go in the garage for the night. At sunset, every night since they arrived, the stupid guy next door opens the front door and calls the cat by name. *"Har Keedie Keedie Keedie."* He will do this for fifteen minutes or until his wife tells him, in a stage whisper, that they are not supposed to have outdoor cats.

I think the cat must believe he is calling someone else named *Keedie* because it never comes *Har.*

When I say Ruth is guarding the little birds, visions of Dranny and her broom lurking about in hopes to find Sylvester may come to mind. Guess again. Modern day Dranny has a small basket on her desk next to the sliding glass door that goes to the deck. On the handle of the basket is a small bow made of pink and white ribbon. Inside the basket you will find six or seven AA batteries. Ruth does not scat cats, she Energizes them.

Rreee...Fthss...THUD!

"Nice catch, Keedie. Go ahead kids, the pool is safe again."

"Wow! That's going to leave a mark. I love you, Baby."

Fifteen minutes later, the doorbell rings. It's Andy and Randy, the grandkids; they are eight and six and live up in Mountainville, just two hours away. They come to visit whenever they can.

"Grandpa, do your neighbors worship frogs? Hee, hee!"

"Yes Andy, I believe they do."

"Don't encourage him, dear," said Ruth.

"Now, Baby, let the boy use his imagination."

"I was talking to him. Andy and Randy and I had a talk about how you fixate on certain things and how they shouldn't get you started on one of your rants."

"Oh."

Andy was right. Our new neighbors in apartment 3G have pushed me about as far as I can be pushed. Now, normally, I am a "live-and-let-live" kind of guy with a soft spot for the little guy. But that little guy in apartment 3G has crossed the line. It seems that these neighbors are the thorn in my side just like Keedie's parents are to Ruth.

We just got rid of the lady that used to sunbathe in the nude in her parking space. She would wait for someone to come by to render aid then jump up with her arms over her head. "Not bad for seventy-two, eh?"

Watching her jump up and down, always seemed to remind me of the fourth grade, when we studied graphic relief maps.

The first thing my new little neighbor did upon moving in was to completely defoliate the small patch of common ground that we shared. Right outside my kitchen window and along the sidewalk from his porch to the now oil stained space where he parked his car. It was necessary for him to saw down a ten foot Juniper tree, cut it into manageable pieces and then throw it into the dumpster across the parking lot.

Then, daily, he would use this now barren spot as a staging area for items that he apparently stole from Fred Sanford on his way home from work.

He started his art project with a concrete Pagoda shaped lantern/ashtray. Within a week he added drift wood, a plastic lattice fence that he erected at the same angle as the ground, about thirty-seven degrees from level, a wrought iron archway, concrete foot prints and frogs.

I never thought there were so many renditions of the frog; statues of frogs in poses, both conceivable and inconceivable, in wood, steel and plaster of Paris. There must have been four dozen frogs standing, jumping and sitting on wooden lily pads.

Well, Andy was right. Frog worship must be going on next door, and as I pointed out to Ruth, if they have that many frogs outside, imagine how many frogs are inside their apartment. I tried to have the manager do something, but I think she belongs to the frog cult also. Andy and Randy and I sneak peeks out the windows and snicker at each frog addition. We never see how they join the others; they just show up as if by magic.

"It must be special frog magic, Grandpa," suggests Randy.

"Maybe we could grab one of them, take it to the garage and make him talk."

"Jack, don't lead them into crime."

"Yeah, that would be Frog-napping, Grandpa."

"I think that is only a crime in Puerto Rico, Andy. In Puerto Rico, people sing songs about frogs, dance frog dances and then at the end of the day they eat frogs and say it tastes like chicken."

"Really? EEW!"

"Well, they don't dance with frogs, Randy."

"Really?"

"No, they can't because the frogs dance like chickens."

"?"

"Look Grandpa, that frog is giving another frog a ride on its back," giggled Randy.

Andy rolled his eyes.

How would he know to roll his eyes? He's only eight. Maybe there was a frog story on the Discovery Channel or he lives near a pond in Mountainville.

HOMEMADE HARMONY

…strum…strum…

"Here's a song I think you oughta know. It's about my penis so it's kinda short…"

…strummm…

"Yay! You're the greatest, Bobby!" someone called out.

I blinked twice and tilted my head to the left. My beer was in my right hand and being supported by my elbow on the bar, it waited for my head to swing back into place.

"Did I hear that right?" I asked the guy next to me. I had been watching my favorite ball team squeak one past the Yankees on the television over the bar. The sound was muted because in a bar nobody listens to a baseball game only football or NASCAR. During my concentration on the game, someone set up a small sound system, two mics and a stool under a blue spot that blinked and flickered with no particular pattern.

"Yeah, HAR, HAR, HAR! That's Bobby Wilson, the "Homemade Cowboy" and it's "Open Mic Night" here at Sparky's. He writes his own songs, he made his own plaid shirt, Hell, he even made his own wrangler's hat out of Shredded Wheat."

It wasn't until the middle of the explanation that I realized the guy next to me must have graduated from the Slim Pickens School of Homemade Cowboy Accents.

"Sorry, I just came in for a beer. I didn't know." I did just come in for a beer. I was waiting for Ruth, my wife, who was grocery shopping across the street. She was going to meet me here when she finished.

"That's okay, Pard, there ain't no sign up to tell ya." My new friend wiped his hand on his homemade jeans and extended it out for me to grasp. I did. He began pumping my arm and stated, "I'm Slim, Slim Perkins."

"Oh,..."I'm Jack..." Was I right or what?

"That's okay; I'll just call ya 'Pard'."

"Okay, Slim."

"Anyways, ole Bobby there, he works over at Krazy Kati's Kraft Korner, ya know, at the Mall. He's the assistant manager of the Notions Department. He gets a discount for all the stuff he needs to make his Cowboy Outfit."

"Oh." Where am I?

There was a small commotion on the small stage. The stage was behind me and to the right; I could see it through the mirror behind the bar. The stage was an area in the corner of the old dance floor that was built before the building was constructed. The bar was actually built around the dance floor which was shipped in from New Orleans, where they say it was part of the stage of a well-known bordello, as I recall the story.

Bobby had a cardboard apple box that he must have used to carry in his electrical equipment. The top section of the box was covered with pieces of straw, glued in place in order to resemble a bale of hay. He rested his feet on this bale as he sat on the stool.

His feet were encased in very obviously homemade cowboy boots. From where I sat, the boots were constructed of newspapers wrapped around his legs and finished off with brown duct tape.

He wore a pair of chaps made of black poster board; they stuck out like rigid bat wings on his legs. His homemade plaid shirt used to be a white shirt that still had the Krazy Kati logo on the pocket. He painted red and black squares on the shirt and tore off the sleeves at the shoulder; around his neck he wore a neckerchief which once was a dinner napkin at Sparky's.

His crown was put together much like the bale of hay, flakes of Shredded Wheat glued onto construction paper. He was truly a homemade cowboy. The sad part of the whole thing was that it was for real. He was serious and it wasn't a joke.

The commotion had to do with a problem in the homemade sound system. It seemed that Bobby was a better hay bale constructor than he was an electrician. When he got too close to the microphone, electricity would arc out of the mic and give his mouth a little blue halo and a one hundred and ten volt kiss. For some reason, he was using high voltage on his sound system, no transformer to step down the power.

BZZZZCK...POP...

"OWW! Dang, it!" Bobby's Yosemite Sam mustache began to smolder, but he could not suppress his art.

...strum...strum...

"...an' on my farm I got my penis. E-I-E-I-O"

...strummm...

"HAR, HAR, HAR!"

"Aint he a hoot?"

"He certainly is something, Slim. He seems to like to sing about his personal parts a lot."

"That's his gimmick. He's got a hundred and fifty homemade songs and he sings 'em all in here every Wednesday night from nine 'til eleven. He wanted to be in here on Thursday, but that's Ladies Night and they don't always git Bobby's sense of humor. Ya know how uppity them girls can git."

"Hmm."

"You see, Pard, ole Bobby writes his own songs."

"That's what you said"

"I didn't just say it Pard, Hell, I meant it! HAR, HAR, HAR! Bobby was gonna go to Memphis to write songs for the Do-It-Yourself Network, but it turned out there wasn't a Krazy Kati's in Memphis, so he couldn't transfer."

"You seem to know a lot about Bobby; you must come in here a lot."

"Ah, Hell no, I'm Bobby's uncle. His ma is my sister, Pearl."

Of course you are, I thought.

"YEOW!"

...BZZZZCK...

The lights dimmed a bit but the little halo got brighter.

"Dang that burns!" came from the stage.

"Hi, honey, I'm ready for my after shopping beer," said Ruth, as she sat in the stool to my right. I moved my cap that I had next to me on the bar to save her a place.

"I don't know, Baby, we might want to think about going home."

"Hey, I just got here. Eww! What smells like someone put out a trash fire with a cat?"

"You'll see."

Ruth shortened her beverage by one inch.

"Howdy, Ma'am, I'm Slim Perkins, it's mighty nice to meet you."

"I thought he was dead," I heard in my right ear.

"No, that was Slim Pickens. Pickens, not Perkins. I tried to warn you," I whispered.

BZZZZCK...strum...strum...

"I was walking with my penis one day, in the merry merry..."

"Check, please!"
"Now, you get it."
We got in the car and sang homemade songs all the way home.

THIRD STREET BAR AND GRILL

"Hold that chicken and make it pea!"

Andy and Randy each covered their mouths with both hands; their eyes were double size with excitement, eyebrows arched as tears shot out of the saucers.

"Did you hear what she said?" Andy giggled through a stage whisper.

Randy was holding an imaginary chicken at arm's length, squeezing his fingers.

"Boys, the waitress is talking about soup," corrected Grandma Ruth, my wife.

"She said pee!" piped Randy. His exuberance made him completely animated.

Andy showed his acceptance of the facts, but looking at his shining eyes, you could tell he appreciated the play on words.

We were out to eat with Andy and Randy, our grandkids, who live two hours away in Mountainville and visit us when they can. Andy and Randy are eight and six respectively.

"The waitress was changing an order with the cook, boys."

I looked over to Ruth, she was smiling broadly. She knew how funny the scene was, but she also had to set a good example for the boys. Not me.

"I hope he washes his hands when he's done!"

"Good one, Grandpa!"

"Boys, don't encourage him."

"Thank you. Andy." Randy was still squeezing the invisible poultry. "Randy, I think your chicken must be dried out by now. No, don't shake it!"

"Jack, see what you started."

Andy smacked himself in the forehead and rolled his eyes.

We all tried to hold it down so that Grandma wouldn't be embarrassed in public, again.

I thought it was one of the funniest things I had ever heard in a restaurant. The humor was being tempered by the fact that this was going to be one of our last meals at one of our favorite spots.

The Third Street Bar and Grill was closing its doors in one week. I should say the Historic Third Street Bar and Grill was closing its doors because TSB&G has been in the same place in our town since 1932. It wasn't always in the same family, but it was always called The Third Street and always in the same place, the first floor of the Spencer Building.

It saw a lot of history in our community. If you took a couple of minutes and didn't mind standing next to strangers while they ate, you could view the past as held by the dozens of black and white photos that lined the dining room and back in the bar section.

The photos were scenes frozen in time from as far back as the early thirties. There were interior shots of patrons and workers long since gone from most memories. Shots from an era when men with large mustaches stood at the bar with one foot on the brass rail, clad in heavy coats and topped with fedoras; spittoons were spaced out on the floor next to the bar. The men held cigars and steins of beer. A display card on the bar featured corn cob pipes for sale.

There were cityscapes of our town with ancient cars and large brick buildings, some of which looked familiar and some not.

The prize of the collection was a shot of the Third Street Bar and Grill on its opening day, March 1st, 1932. It was an exterior view from the street of the small door to the left of the large window that rested on a brick veneer front. "Third Street Bar and Grill" was hand painted on the pane in an arc that took up most of the sixteen feet of glass. Standing in front of the three story building were three men with bow ties and garters on their sleeves and three young girls in uniforms, aprons and white caps, pride and anxiety shown in their faces.

We frequently took the boys there for Saturday morning breakfast. If business was slow, I would take the boys around to view the past, pointing out the old fire trucks and police cars in the picture of a parade in front of the old office buildings and shops of downtown on St. Patrick's day.

All of the history paled in comparison to the gigglefest we experienced that day, which made losing a friend like Third Street a little easier.

Losing their lease caused the old girl to be put down. It was very confusing not knowing all of the particulars, but at a time when everyone is trying to keep local businesses in business to have the rent raised beyond budgeting, seemed to be a black time in our history.

Chemistry has as much to do with a good business as location. The Third Street had both. Bobby, Brenda and DeWayne were the standards other cafes should have shot for when putting together a winning crew. Good food, good service and humor were offered at every visit.

On the way back home we explained to the boys why we wouldn't be able to eat there on their next visit. They were sad but seemed to understand. A few of their favorite places in Mountainville may have gone away also.

When we returned home, the boys had forgotten about Third Street and were on to other interests, Pokeman cards and TV.

It will be a while for me.

A TRIP TO THE PSYCHIC

"I see you work hard for a living, Senor," her dark eyes gleamed as she looked up from my hands.

I don't really think she was out on a limb with her statement like she tried to make it sound. My hands were as dry and rough as Mojave Park. La Senora Gomez, the Psychic Palm-Reader, knew how to put on a good show. Ambiance will help to reassure the susceptible, and her place was chock full of ambiance.

Walking in from the street, you would see a small neon sign in the shape of a hand in the window. Printed on the inside of the electric pink outline were the words: "PSYCHIC PALM READER."

As we entered the converted two story house, a bead curtain separated the alcove and the front room. The front room was "lit" by a floor lamp on either side of the room. The lamps must have been plugged into a rheostat in order to lower the output of the bulbs to twenty-two and a half watts each. They both wore faded shades with most of the fringe pieces still attached.

On the right side of the room was a glass fronted case. Inside the case were dozens of apothecary jars filled with dark colored substances both solid and liquid. On top of the case were larger glass jars with what appeared to be various dried animal parts; paws, tails, wings and beaks. All of the jars wore time yellowed labels with roman numerals hand printed with red ink to indicate a coded system of inventory control. It had everything necessary to put you in the mood for magic.

On the left side of the room were three overstuffed chairs that sat side by side. Centered on the top of the back of each were white lace trimmed antimacassars, none of them matched each other. The lamp stood in the near corner and ruled over those who would sit below.

Straight ahead was a wall with two doors. A large picture of Jesus hung in the space between the doors. It was the picture of Jesus, palms together, looking up as if He was trying to remember where he left his keys. Perhaps he came here to have La Senora help him divine their location, and she took his picture for her trouble. The odor of petiole and sandalwood filled the air to the point that for a minute I thought that the picture might have been that of an old English professor I had in college. His name was George.

Below the picture was a pedestal with a statue of Jesus. It was the pose of Him with his hands spread apart. I looked for the caption card that would report that famous quote: "I caught a fish this big!" I always wondered if He was the patron saint of fishing exaggerations.

I was at the Psychic Palm Reader's studio/shop with my friend DeWayne. I told him that I would accompany him for a reading even though he understood I held no faith in the "Art."

DeWayne was having trouble with his girlfriend, Brenda. Ever since she got her new job as a secretary with the state motor pool, she seemed to be more distant. She kept breaking dates with him and seemed to be letting herself go in the appearance department. DeWayne was emotional and always could read more into a situation than anyone I knew.

"Look at her! She used to be so sexy and wore sexy clothes. Now she wears sweatpants!" Because he was almost crying, I agreed to go with him to see the seer.

We sat in the large chairs in the front room and waited for La Senora Gomez. DeWayne sat with his hands on his knees. He strummed his fingers in time with the Mexican music that we could hear from behind the left door. It reminded me that the oom-pah beat of most Mexican tunes is the same as a good German Polka.

DeWayne's eyes were wide but instead of taking in more scenery, he just stared straight ahead. He was practicing his questions to the fortune teller.

"You'll be just fine, DeWayne. I'll tell you what," I said calmly, "I'll go first."

Just then the left door opened; there was no music coming out of the open door. From behind the door was darkness. Into the dimly lit room glided a small framed, white haired woman. Wearing a flowing white dress and a dark brown cross held around her neck with a brown string. She looked like the ghost of a small child.

"*Buenos dias*, I am Imelda Gomez. How can I help you today?" She offered her hand; I took it and she led me down the hallway to the door on the right. She opened the door and I held it open for her to lead the way.

When I entered the room, I was impressed. For as dim as the ante room was, this room was fifty times brighter than a normal room. My eyes hurt when I was exposed to the brightness. The walls were covered with layers of white material which defused the light which must have shown up from the floor and down from the ceiling along the walls. The sheet like material obscured the location of walls and even the corners of the room. The floor was covered with a white carpet, but the ceiling was a pale blue.

In the middle of this faux cloud was a small round table. A red table cloth touched the floor all around the three foot high, four foot round circle. A high backed wooden chair was placed at three o'clock and another at six.

Missing from this divine look-alike were the things I thought would be standard equipment; no candles, no crystal ball, no gypsy music. In fact there was no music at all. From nowhere specifically you could hear wind blowing. When I said I was impressed, I should have said completely impressed. At this point I knew DeWayne was going to be a dead duck. I was a non-believer and my mouth was dry from being wide open for the last two minutes.

We sat in the chairs. She examined my right hand and made her opening statement. I told her she was correct. She smiled a kind knowing smile.

"I know why you are here, *mi hijo.*"

"Oh, really?" I tried not to sound too smug.

"You are a non-believer, but you care for your friend. You think because he has problems, he will be taken advantage of by me and by others. You are a good friend. He is lucky to have you. I am impressed to see how much heart you have."

"Thank you. You have a very impressive place here. You see very clearly, which is impressive also. What is your plan for my friend?"

"I can tell he has love problems. He doubts his love is returned. He is young and needs his love returned, yes?"

"You are very good. How do you know these things?"

"Remember the sign on your way in?"

"What are you going to tell him?"

"The truth, *mi hijo,* the truth."

"Be gentle, please."

She smiled broadly.

I returned to the ante room. DeWayne's eyes got big.

"It'll be fine, Buddy," I said.

Thirty minutes later, DeWayne returned.

"Well?"

"I'll tell you in the car," said my friend.

On the way back home, DeWayne almost burst. "She was amazing! She knew everything!"

"Are you going to be okay?"

"She told me I was looking for returned love. After I told her my Brenda worked for the state motor pool, she said the same thing happened to her daughter. Not to worry, she told me, she joined the state workers' union. They have meetings every month after work. To ensure a good attendance, the leaders serve pies and cakes. She's not growing away from me, she just growing. I guess it happens a lot."

A HAPPY HALLOWEEN

"A ninja."

"No."

"Not a ninja?"

"No, I mean, yes!"

"A crow?"

"No."

"A domino?"

"No."

"Felix the Cat?"

"No."

"A nun."

"What?"

"Okay, Randy, you're wearing all black, what are you dressed as?"

"A ninja!"

Grrrr.

I knew better than getting into a guessing game with a six year old.

Andy and Randy were down for the weekend. They are eight and six respectively and live in Mountainville about two hours from here and they stop by when they can. They stopped by to show us their Halloween costumes.

Apparently, Randy is going to be a ninja, but Andy was holding his disguise as a secret.

"Andy, do you have a costume?" asked Ruth, my wife. She could see that he was holding something back when he arrived.

"No, not yet. Could you help me, Grandma?"

"Why, yes, of course!" volunteered Grandma. "What are you thinking of?"

"Pssss pssss pssss pssss, pssss pssss."

"We'll have to go to the garage, dear. Jack, could you put together some lunch, please?"

"Yes, of course."

"Andy and I will be out there the rest of the day."

"Is there anything I can help you with?" My curiosity began to get the better of me.

"Oh, no, I've got it."

She's got it? My garage? My tools? And I'm making lunch?   Grrrr.

"What's for lunch, Grandpa?"

"Ninja burgers."

"Really?"

I took two sandwiches and glasses of milk out to the garage and handed them through the slightly opened door, after I knocked.

I heard a muffled, "Thank you, Grandpa!"

For the next four hours I heard sawing, hammering, drilling and more hammering. Meanwhile, I watched Ewoks or something on TV with Johnny Cash.

At four-thirty the front door opened and in walked Ruth. She brushed her hands together in a triumphant fashion then opened her palms with a flourish like a black-jack dealer making change or the hand signal the bellman gives to the crane operator when he's done with a pick.

"I think we are done for today."

"You sure were making a lot of noise out there. What have you two been up to?"

"We were making Andy's costume. Would you like to see it?"

"Yes, I would."

In walked a four foot high character from one of my favorite TV shows, Bender, the robot from Futurama.

From the top of his antenna to the bottom of his round feet, it was Bender in the flesh, or, should I say, in the sheet metal.

"Ta Daa...Kiss my shiny butt!"

Ruth and Andy created a perfect replica of a cartoon character. I was very impressed; dryer vent arms and legs, goggles and an actual door that opened in the front. I was not only impressed but a bit envious, I could have done it, but I was proud of Ruth and the fact that it only took four hours was commendable. I probably would have taken longer.

Before the sun set, we had two totally ready to haunt trick-or-treaters on their way through the neighborhood. Ruth and I carried flashlights and provided protection, not that it was needed. When we returned, Bender and Paladin each had a bucketful of candy.

It was a happy Halloween.

- -

ONE NIGHT ACROSS TOWN

We went to a not so customary bar last week to watch a pool tournament that involved some friends of ours. Let me rephrase, to a Pool League contest. I guess there is quite a difference.

My wife, Ruth, and I are new-comers to the pool scene. We don't play but we do enjoy watching a good contest.

The boys from our favorite bar, Sparky's, were playing against their arch enemies who are sponsored by Spanky's. I know, what are the odds?

Spanky's is a medium sized bar that has more pool tables than regular tables. We hadn't been there since we got spooked the last time we went there, two years ago. Spanky's is in a pretty scary part of town, but not many scary people go there because it's in a pretty scary part of town, remember?

The members of the opposing team looked a lot like the members of our team. Only it is obvious our team knew how to do laundry or at least knew someone who did.

We arrived prior to the contest to visit with our friend Dexter, who was captain of the team. He introduced us to the rest of the guys: Tommy, Rich, Ed and Spit. Spit is the alternate player, kind of like the vice president, "a heartbeat away" from officially being on the team.

I asked Spit, who works as mechanic at the Ford dealership, how he got his unusual nickname.

"Not from chewing tobacco," he said with a broad smile to demonstrate the perfect white teeth of which he was very proud. "My mom says she was always telling me to spit something or other out of my mouth, so she

shortened the order down to just the one word, 'Spit."
After a while, I guess I heard it so much that I started to
respond to it and it stuck."

Ed and Rich worked together with Dexter at Home
Depot where Dexter works as a shift manager. He
arranged it so the boys got the night off to play in the pool
tournament. We knew Dexter from our occasional stops
for beer at Sparky's. Dexter is a very affable and outgoing
young man who has an encyclopedic knowledge of US
History. He is very impressive.

"When you're a skinny, little black kid, like I was in
high school, you had to be good at something," he would
always say, using his self-deprecating sense of humor to
apologize for his intelligence.

Tommy is Tommy La Fountaine, the famous
author and entertainment reporter who lives in our town
and can be read in forty-eight newspapers in the US and
Canada. He specializes in covering bands and music
trends. He is frequently quoted and sometimes seen on
MTV. He used to be in a boy-band in the eighties but
gave up the business after an accident cost him two
finger tips so he could not play the guitar again. He still
has the frail frame that made him the darling of his fans,
but his long flowing hair is now restricted to the back of
his head, not the top. I had seen him before, just enough
to smile at and nod to and I had heard him talking down
the bar several times.

"Are you a pool player?" ask Tommy.

"No, not me, we just know some of the guys on
the team."

"Didn't I see you at Sparky's on open mic night
last month?"

"You could have. Ruth, my wife, goes shopping across the street and I wait for her at Sparky's sometimes."

"It was the night Bobby Wilson was singing."

"Oh yeah, The Home-made Cowboy."

"What did you think?"

"I'm not the music expert here; what did you think?"

"I loved him! I wrote a two pager for Back Beat Magazine all about him and his home made music."

"I thought he was a little one dimensional with his personal parts song themes."

"That's his gimmick!"

"I thought his gimmick was that he made his own cowboy suit."

"Well, that too!"

"Personally, I didn't like him. I'm not a music snob; I like all kinds of music, just not his."

"What do think about 'Alternative Rock'?" He was testing me.

"I like a lot of the music that came out of the nineties," I replied. "But I always thought if there were more guys like Kurt Cobain, eventually there would be less guys like Kurt Cobain."

Tommy La Fountaine sneered at me and turned around to talk to someone else.

Ruth came over from the bar to our table with two beers. Our friend, Dexter, was getting ready to start a game with one of the only other black guys in our town, the guy I recognized as the man who works at the place where I buy gas, George Washington.

I enjoy buying gas from George because he always refers to himself in the third person; this made the trash-talking part of the game very interesting. At the coin toss to determine who broke, I could hear, "George Washington is going to kick your ass, son."

"What?" questioned Dexter, who obviously bought his gas somewhere else.

"George Washington is going to take you to school, son," he spoke with a smooth, quiet voice that resembled Marvin Gaye.

It was at this time that I could hear a commotion behind me and heard Ruth say. "Oh, my!"

I slowly turned to my left. I always turn slowly in a strange bar; it's much safer that way. I now saw what Ruth was witnessing. I thought someone was carrying a road map into the bar and then my eyes focused. We were staring at the back of a woman who had taken off her shirt to show off her tattooed back. Oh, my!

It seems that Brenda, one of the strippers from Winkie's across the street, came in and was detailing all of the ink on her back. Winkie's is the strip bar where more experienced dancers work, or as the locals say, "Wrinkles is where old strippers go to die."

"Is she topless?" I asked.

"Apparently so."

"Dr. Franco is done working on me," declared Brenda to Ruth. "He did my front last year, see," she said. She posed, shirtless, with her left hand in the air while bringing her right down in front of herself with a flourish much like that model on "The Price is Right" when she shows off a new refrigerator. Ten thousand dollars' worth of silicone and suture gave this fifty year old woman the body of a forty-eight year old. And Winkie's gave her a way to pay off her new additions; there must be dozens of men in our town who haven't seen her breasts in the last thirty years of her dancing

121

career and who are willing to pay good money to see them now.

We were faced with a social dilemma. Should we stare at her offering or turn our head which might show that we didn't appreciate all of her work. Hmmm. We decided to take turns at looking and not looking. It was funny, we figured out this part without even discussing it.

Then she spun around, "This year, Dr. Franco did my back!" she held her arms outstretched and looked back at us over her shoulder. She displayed an entire work of tattoo art/fanaticism; almost every square inch of her back was covered with ink. "Check it out! I spent ten K on the front and twelve on the back."

"Oh, yeah," we said in unison.

Two things became evident; first, we seemed to be the only people she was talking to, then, no one seemed to care there was a half-naked lady in the bar. The regulars at Spanky's must be accustomed to seeing Brenda, almost all of her, all the time.

We began inspecting the human mural. The multi-colored canvas came into focus and revealed a representation of the Revolutionary War. Everything related to the time was there to be seen; the signing of the Declaration of Independence, Old North Church, Breed's Hill, George Washington atop a white horse and scores of British soldiers in their cardinal red uniforms and American soldiers in both dark blue and buckskin uniforms. Everything from muskets firing to canons blasting could be seen on the woman's back. It was even more impressive than the front view.

I motioned for Dexter to stop by to do a quick fact check. After we got Brenda to quit wiggling, Dexter spent about five minutes examining the collage, "I only see a couple errors."

"Really?"

"I told you Dr. Franco does good work."

"The Declaration of Independence is short one signature; it only has fifty-five names. It's missing Carter Braxton, but that is easy to forgive because his is the one on bottom of the list and he needed to have more room for Hancock. The thing I can't overlook is I know Mighty Mouse was not in the Revolution." He pointed to a spot just above her waist in the center of her back. He was right; there was Mighty Mouse with his hands on his hips, musket balls were turning to dust as they struck his Mighty Chest.

"There he is to save the day!" I almost sang it out.

"Mighty Mouse is Dr. Franco's hero; he puts him in all of his works." She turned around and hefted her major attractions. "Of course, he didn't put Mighty Mouse on the girls. That would be tacky."

"That *would* be tacky." I agreed.

Maybe feeling a chill, Brenda put on her black Winkie's tee shirt, putting an end to the show. As she went to the other side of the bar, Dexter followed closely behind. I asked Ruth if she thought that amount of weight under one's skin could affect one's balance.

"I'm sure every time she falls down, she lands on her back."

"You know, Ruth," I chortled, "you could take what you said two different ways."

"No, just one."

- -

MAYA PREDICTIONS

Most people overlook the obvious connections to things in history and nature as we know it. I am not an alarmist nor am I a conspiracy nut. I do, however, have a knack for seeing connections in our life. Not unlike a younger James Burke, I see how thing are or at least could be linked together if you squint your eyes just right.

I took many history classes in college. Several dealt with the history of the Americas, not modern but pre-Columbian. I learned all I could about the Mayans, the greatest civilization in the history of civilization. The Mayans, their culture, their science, their people, their religion and their disappearance all combined into the mystery of their hemisphere.

Snakes, jaguars, parrots and monkeys represented religious symbols in their artwork but my favorite deity in the Mayan religion was *Chacmool*, the Mayan rain god.

The reclining figure looks as though he's calling back to his mom, "No, I'm not masturbating again. Yes, I'm sure." Although he probably really was masturbating and why not, he was a god.

Today, I can't help but draw lines between the Mayan calendar stoppage (end of the world) and key signs in our culture today as to the verification of their estimate of the third week in December of 2012 as the end of the world. Look at the picture for yourself.

Lying back, unconcerned, wearing his cowboy boots and funny hat, who does Chacmool really look like, someone whose obituary is being written today in our national news?

Twinkie the Kid, the Chacmool of our day, died last week. Like many anthropologists believe, Twinkie the Kid also outgrew his environment. His natural resources could no longer sustain his needs and he and his fellow gods, King Ding Dong, Happy Ho Ho, Captain Cupcake and Fruit pie the Magician mysteriously disappeared just like the Maya and their religious icons.

The Mayans saw the future and knew the importance of the signs of the time. For ninety-five years Twinkie and the boys ruled the commercial world that we live in. With their passing, there goes the capitalistic system as we know it. The end of the world is at hand and I think it just may be on December 21, 2012 as predicted by the Mayan calendar, the day the last Twinkie was produced.

More Opic Observations

- -

Also by Jack Haines
At
Rogue Phoenix Press

My Opic Observations

I admittedly have a different interpretation on how things work in my world. I have been told I am sanctimonious, sarcastic and irreverent. Another ex-wife said I was cruel and hypercritical. The truth is I have a large number of soft spots and whenever I see a naked Emperor, I have to scream out. I have a particular weakness for the pompous and those who fear sunlight. No, not vampires. Writing helps relieve the sting from the head slapping after I witness my fellow humans in their environment.

Special Notice!

Most of this book is at least 95% true; the rest is over 100%